MW01122532

PUT THE GADGET GURU TO WORK FOR YOU!

There are so many new kinds of TVs and VCRs out there . . . which one is best for my family?

From TV speakers, big screens, and home satellite systems to the newest cutting-edge technology, the Guru helps you put together the home theater system that's right for you.

Is a big-name computer better than the one my next-door neighbor pieced together in his basement?

For reliability, value, and service, the Guru shows you where to get the most machine for your buck—and which ones to avoid.

I keep hearing about the DVD player. What is it—and should I get one?

The Guru explains the hottest new product of the year, and the make and model you should buy.

I love espresso. But those machines scare me. Do they work?

Don't get steamed at your cappuccino maker. The Guru knows which one delivers the goods—and which ones aren't worth beans.

The Gadget Guru's Guide to the Best

ALSO BY ANDY PARGH

*The Gadget Guru's Make-It-Easy
Guide to Home Repair*

ANDY PARGH
WITH JOHN KELLEY

WARNER BOOKS

A Time Warner Company

The information provided in this book is based upon sources that the authors believe to be reliable. All such
information regarding individual products and companies is current as of May 1997.

Copyright © 1997 by Andy Pargh
All rights reserved.
Warner Books, Inc., 1271 Avenue of the Americas,
New York, NY 10020
Visit our Web site at http://www.warnerbooks.com

 A Time Warner Company

First Printing: December 1997

10 9 8 7 6 5 4 3 2 1

Library of Congress Cataloging-in-Publication Data

Pargh, Andy.
    The Gadget guru's guide to the best / Andy Pargh, with John
Kelley.
        p. cm.
    Includes index.
    ISBN 0-446-67323-4
    1. Home economics—Equipment and supplies—Evaluation.
2. Household appliances, Electric—Evaluation. 3. Consumer goods—
Evaluation. I. Kelley, John. II. Title
TX298.P36 1997
381.3'3—dc21   97-24331
                                                              CIP

Book design & text composition by L&G McRee
Cover design by Tony Russo

To Larry and Roofer:
two of the best.

Acknowledgments

Compiling the information in this book has truly been a labor of love. We had to work months in advance to deliver timely and accurate information, and to rely on countless manufacturers to make us privy to information that they would rather have kept close to the vest. Without the support and trust of the various manufacturers and their public relations representatives this book would not have been possible.

To Jamie Raab and John Aherne of Warner Books, who not only believed in this concept but who made it one of the most rewarding projects my company has ever taken on. I am truly fortunate to have these two folks running the front lines and constantly giving us the support needed to accomplish our tasks.

To John Lentz, my friend, partner, attorney, and agent, who has never stopped believing in me and who has earned the respect of his legal peers in the publishing, syndication, and television worlds. His never-say-die attitude has earned him the nickname "The Captain," as he never abandons the ship.

To the Gadget Guru staff, the folks behind the scenes who make sure that our syndicated newspaper column, NBC *Today* show segments, magazine articles, Internet services, America Online forum, and never-ending list of new projects keep going and going and going. To Terri, my personal assistant, who constantly keeps track of where I have to be and when I have to be there and makes sure that I get back and forth to the airport on time and in one piece.

To Roland Woerner of the *Today* show, who believed in me from the start.

And finally, and most important, to my co-author, John Kelley, who burned the midnight oil for months on end in order for us to accomplish our dream of delivering to the world this book. John, you can now go home to your wife, Melissa, and play with Anna and Nathan! John and I have worked together for more years than I care to remember. Although he can still make a killer Café Sperry (a wild drink from his bartending years), he has become the best new products researcher and editor in the business.

Introduction

I've said this often: Andy Pargh has the greatest job in the world—and I'm jealous!

I've worked with Andy for the past two years on the weekend edition of the *Today* show and have joked with him regularly about what he does for a living: plays with toys! But what separates Andy from the pack, and makes his work both enjoyable and educational, is that he does more than just order products and demonstrate them on the air. He carefully tests these items and gives our audience an honest view of how they work and if they are worth the money. With all the advertising hype these days, our viewers know that they can turn to Andy for a fair look at the newest and most interesting products on the market.

What truly amazes me is the broad range of products and services he covers. On any Saturday you can tune in and see Andy effortlessly taking the mystery out of buying a computer, a VCR, or a camera, as well as see him demonstrating the latest in personal watercraft, motorcycles, or snow skiing gear. You might even see him strapped in a roller coaster and zooming along at 90 mph.

He not only tests these products, he lives the lifestyle—so much so that if he were not getting paid by NBC he'd probably pay us! He truly loves his job, and it shows.

I was honored when Andy asked me to write this introduction since, over the years, we have become not just colleagues but also good friends.

Each and every week he brings to our show enthusiasm, integrity, and a great wit that our viewers have come to respect and enjoy.

With Andy, new products are his life. As I have often stated: When I grow up, I want to be Andy Pargh!

—JACK FORD
Chief Legal Correspondent
NBC News

Contents

CHAPTER **5.** Sporting Goods 191

CHAPTER **6.** Big Toys for Aging Boomers 203

Best New Roller Coaster: Superman the Escape
Best New Concept Ride: SkyCoaster
Best Burger: In N Out
Best Las Vegas Hotel: Caesars Palace
Best Products for the Recycle Bin

Phone Contacts 265

CHAPTER 1

Consumer Electronics

Whether you're tapping your alarm clock's snooze button for a few more minutes' sleep, using a cordless telephone to talk while walking around the house, watching the *Today* show on a big-screen television, or depending on a VCR to record your favorite sitcom, consumer electronic products are a major part of our daily routines.

Life hasn't always been so easy.

Remember the days before the VCR? We used to have to rush home in order to watch our favorite show. What about life before the telephone answering machine? If people needed to get in contact with you, they would have to continue calling until they could catch you at home. Remember when we had to actually answer the phone, not just monitor the machine to hear who was calling?

These days, with such an abundant selection of products available, it can be difficult, if not downright confusing, trying to select the right television, answering machine, cordless phone, or VCR for our lifestyles.

That's what this chapter is all about: helping you make educated choices in the confusing world of consumer electronics.

For more than twenty years, the changing trends of consumer electronics have been my life. Straight out of college I worked for my brother's company selling calculators to major department stores. I then became a territorial manager for Texas Instruments and marketed the first digital watch for under ten dollars. Then, as a product manager at Panasonic, our group took the answering machine from the specialty catalog and made it affordable enough to leap off the shelves at discount stores. At Uniden, I witnessed the transformation of the two-way radio into the ever-popular cordless telephone.

In 1984, armed with the knowledge of an insider, I defected to the other side of the fence and became a consumer reporter. I have since created the nation's largest (circulation-wise, that is) new product reporting organization.

As a reporter, I covered just about every major change of the consumer electronics industry. The subjects ranged from the controversial Beta versus VHS war in the early '80s to the introduction and mass-marketing of the compact disc. Needless to say, reporting on this industry has never been boring. Products keep getting better and less expensive, making the consumer the ultimate winner.

In 1975 a 25-inch family room television cost $1,000 to $1,700. Today, you can buy a 27-inch model that includes features not even dreamed about back then, for $650. Imagine if the automakers of the world had followed the path led by the electronics manufacturers: We'd be driving $10,000 Cadillacs, and they would get 100 miles per gallon!

The year 1997 brought to the market a plethora of items seeking to become a part of our everyday lives: new telephones that surf the Internet, clocks that automatically set themselves, televisions with clearer pictures, video telephones that bring people together, and a revolutionary new home movie playback format called DVD.

Yet all that glitters is not gold. A lot of wading and sifting through the products is necessary to find those that truly deliver a balance of features and functions worthy of our hard earned dollars.

By separating fact from fiction and weeding through the maze, my co-author, John Kelley, and I have tediously sought and assembled for your pleasure the consumer electronics products we believe to be the best of 1997.

BEST NEW TECHNOLOGY: THE DIGITAL VERSATILE DISC, OR DVD

With more scrapped launch dates than an experimental NASA rocket, the digital versatile disc, or DVD, has been something of an enigma.

However, 1997 was the year that this revolutionary new video playback format became a reality.

DVDs are compact disc look-alikes that, instead of playing back a mere 74 minutes of music, deliver up to 133 minutes of motion pictures on a single disc. DVD video quality far exceeds that of VHS tapes and even puts the tried-and-true high-quality laser disc to shame. But other than just offering another pretty picture, it is also bringing to life a new audio format called Dolby Digital (see page 42 for explanation) that, when connected to the right equipment, can truly bring the theater experience to your home.

DVDs also have previously unheard-of functions such as parental controls that, with a press of a button, allow you to remove graphic violence and sexual content from selected movie titles; of course if you attempted to watch G-rated versions of *Pulp Fiction* or *Terminator*, each would probably run only 18 minutes or so. DVDs also allow the user to view movies with multiple aspect ratios like the wide-screen letterbox format and have a choice of up to eight different language preferences. Some titles will even include special director's cut sequences, which will allow the user to select different camera angles and multiple story endings.

Of course, to take advantage of this new technology you have to purchase a DVD player. Now the bad news: Since current DVDs do not yet record, they are basically useless without DVD software, and it is impossible for Hollywood to transform entire inventories of movies onto the DVD format overnight. It will take a while to have a wide assortment of movies available for purchase—and even longer to see an abundant supply at the neighborhood video store. Even without extensive movie libraries, the DVD player will be the ultimate conversation piece of 1997. However, it will most likely not be a major "must have" for most consumers for a few more years. But because of its superior audio and video qualities, I believe that Hollywood will embrace this format and it will quickly become the in-home movie-viewing format of choice. This will in turn make the DVD as common as the VCR in the years to come, and when they market a recordable/erasable DVD (expected by the year 2000), the VCR tape's days are numbered. In the meantime, for all you early adopters and videophiles, I've provided a quick buying guide and the best DVD players on the market.

DVD GLOSSARY

Horizontal resolution: Industry video measurement that helps determine picture quality. DVDs deliver 500 lines of horizontal resolution (the best in the business). For comparison here are the other video devices:

Standard VHS VCR: 240 lines of horizontal resolution
Super VHS VCR: 400 lines of horizontal resolution
Laser disc player: 430 lines of horizontal resolution

S-video jack: Standard on all DVDs. It is a superior video-only output that allows you (if your TV has an S-video input) to connect the DVD player to your TV with a $5 S-video cable, instead of with the standard jacks. S-video jacks enable you to get the best video signal out of the DVD.

Best Entry-Level DVD Player: RCA Model No. 5200P

$600

With enough features to get you into this exciting format at a price that won't pinch too much, this model from RCA is a perfect entry-level machine.

Definitely the best value for a full-function DVD player, this model packs many of the more desirable features of higher-end players in a nice, tidy package. Included is a Dolby Digital audio output, an option that allows for the connection to a compatible high-end Dolby Digital stereo receiver for theater-like sound. Other features include CD audio playback, parental controls, and a dual-sided function that will double the playback time to 266 minutes on future DVD discs.

It delivers 480 lines of horizontal resolution (as compared to 240 lines for a standard VHS VCR) and includes both S-video and digital outputs. Purchasers of other RCA products will appreciate the look-alike cosmetics that match RCA's VCR and digital satellite systems (DSS).

Best Step-Up DVD Player: Toshiba Model No. SD-3006

$700

Whenever a new technology is introduced, there is always one company that stakes its claim as its inventor and champion. With DVD, it is Toshiba.

When DVD was first announced, the folks at Toshiba gave speech after speech, party after party, and spent megabucks trying to convince the press and the world that the DVD was "its" format. Although they successfully convinced some, many skeptics including myself became Toshiba's adversaries and gave its PR folks many a Maalox moment. That's because of the obvious lack of support the DVD format was getting from Hollywood.

Although Toshiba officials promised to be the first to deliver and have DVD players in stores in time for the all-important 1996 holiday season, they and the other DVD manufacturers underestimated Hollywood's resolve and no players were marketed until well into 1997. But this was probably a good thing, because if they had, there would not have been a single DVD movie (except for the demo disc that came in the box) available for purchase.

Finally, Toshiba was able to introduce a model that John and I feel really delivers the goods.

It features up to 500 lines of resolution, parental controls, audio CD playback, and a pair of audio outputs for Dolby Digital. For the home theater aficionado this DVD also has component video outputs. These provide greatly enhanced picture quality (with an appropriate TV set or projector) and allow you to add high-end devices called line scanning converters (otherwise known as doublers, quadruplers) that give you the ultimate in picture quality. Other features include S-video jacks, a universal remote control, and, for the video purist, gold-plated jacks, which provide the ultimate in viewing satisfaction.

What really separates this unit from the pack is its ability to use advanced special effects on selected DVD titles, allowing the user to view the film from the camera angle of his or her choice, to use freeze-frame, and to go in for close-ups.

Best Feature on a DVD: Pioneer DVD700 DVD/LD

$1,000

Initially, with only a few hundred DVD movie titles available in stores compared to more than 10,000 of their VHS tape counterparts, who is going to go out and invest in a DVD player? The early adopter, that's who.

Everybody knows them. They are the first on the block with everything. They are also the ones we want as friends, as they usually don't hold on to their equipment too long and will make you a sweet deal to buy their older thingamajig so that they can buy the latest model. They are also the ones who will come over and patiently show us how to use our new "toys."

When it comes to DVD, the best-thinking award goes to Pioneer for recognizing that today's laser disc owner is probably an early DVD adopter. For that reason, Pioneer created the world's first combination laser disc/DVD player. It's two, two, two movie players in one!

It features Dolby Digital optical and digital outputs, separate DVD and laser disc trays, two S-video outputs, Dolby Digital RF output for laser disc, digital memory for videodisc playback, an on-screen graphical user interface, 500 lines of resolution, and a remote control. Like all DVD players it plays audio CDs as well.

Best Overall DVD Player: Sony DVP-S7000

$1,000

Targeting the audio enthusiast as well as the video lover, Sony's unit offers state-of-the-art CD technology to go along with its DVD playback capabilities.

Featuring a 10-bit digital-to-analog converter (which provides for a clear, crisp picture by eliminating those little white dots that appear on many videos), the Sony unit also incorporates a separate processor chip that drives a feature called smooth scan. This allows viewers to seamlessly view movies or music videos in high speed (fast-forward or reverse), slow motion, or frame by frame.

Other features include both component and composite video outputs that allow you to bypass the TV's built-in decoder for a less processed, hence better, picture. The Dolby Digital audio output is further enhanced by Sony's digital cinema sound fields and bass redirection functions that, through an on-screen graphic equalizer, can be adjusted for optimal listening.

For audio CD playback, it includes a digital filter for high music resolution and a dual discrete optical pickup feature that uses two different lasers to recognize the difference between a DVD (which is thicker) and a CD for optimized tracking for whichever disc you are using.

Ultimate DVD Player: Faroudja DVD1000

$5,500

If money is not an issue and you're looking to buy the same DVD player that will be adorning the shelves of the Spielbergs and Lucases of the world, look no further than this model from Faroudja.

Featuring built-in low noise and high linearity video circuitry, the

Faroudja player enhances DVD's already superb video quality by extensively processing the picture before it hits your screen. Forgetting the "technojargon," quite simply this DVD delivers the crispest, best-looking pictures on the market.

Audiowise, the unit has both Dolby Digital and DTS (which stands for digital theater system—an audio format that is different from Dolby's that many audio aficionados prefer) surround sound decoders.

Other features include state-of-the-art connections including RGB/YUV switchable video outputs, which, in layman's terms, means you can bypass the color decoder on your TV for a better picture; a heavy gauge; vibration-resistant chassis; and a remote control. Of course with a price tag of over $5,000, you pay to play.

TELEVISIONS

Buying a television is not a fun experience. With today's superstores carrying such a large array of different models, it is confusing to select just the right one for you. And that's just what the retailers want: for you to be confused. Televisions are displayed in a method that forces you to see the ones that the store management is pushing. It is truly both an art and a science. The models that they want you to buy are given an advantageous position in the store, and the pictures are adjusted to look better (i.e., brighter). The sets they don't want you to consider, maybe because they are making a smaller profit margin, are placed in less favorable locations.

Most television stores are designed to put you, the potential buyer, in a position of requiring sales assistance. And believe me, it is easier to find a salesperson in a television store than a flounder in a fish market. Although these hardworking folks are there to help, their mission in life is to not let you leave without making a purchase. And, hopefully, make you spend more than you'd planned. In salesperson speak, they want you to *show them the money!* But that's their job. And if you are armed with the right questions, a salesperson can be a valuable resource.

Unless you walk into a store knowing the exact make and model of television you want, or at least have a basic knowledge of what you are looking for, you are at the mercy of the salesperson. Today's televisions are so loaded with features that they can appear to do everything but walk the dog.

Rule number one in buying a new television set is to not be intimidated by the variety of sets on display. Another good rule of thumb is to know how much you want to spend and then stick to your budget. Also, know where the TV is going to be placed in your room at home and with what furniture it's going to be placed.

The good news is that, like the telephone, today's televisions are one of the most reliable, dependable products on the planet. Unlike computers, televisions don't have to be upgraded every six months just to operate properly. This brings up another point. There is an entirely new television technology a year or so away called HDTV (high definition television), so should you buy a new television today, or wait for this new technology?

I say buy. That's because, unless your name is Rockefeller (or Gates) and price is no object, the initial HDTVs will be more expensive. Also, like when the first color televisions surfaced on the market, it will take a while for the TV networks and affiliates to begin a full schedule of HDTV broadcasting.

For those not familiar, HDTVs are a new format that feature a rectangular viewing surface that mimics the "wide-screen" aspect ratio of a movie theater. The picture quality is roughly four times that of a standard television, which have nearly square picture tubes. In simple terms, the picture quality is so clear, it is more like looking out a window than staring at the boob tube. When HDTVs hit the market as early as 1998, prices will be steep, with initial models selling for between $8,000 and $10,000.

But as I said before, if you need a new television now, buy it now. Just be aware that this new format is being readied for the marketplace.

Here's a quick TV primer and our picks for the best televisions of the year:

There are essentially two types of television sets: direct view and projection.

- Direct-view sets have glass screens with a large picture tube inside. The maximum direct size you can purchase is a 40-inch. (Note: all screen sizes are measured diagonally.) Direct-view sets are usually clearer, brighter, and more defined than projections, but pictures cannot be as large.
- Projection sets use three picture tubes or LCD panels that project the picture on a screen. They start in size where direct-view models leave off, and are available in tabletop or stand-alone sizes up to 80-inches diagonally.

Tip: Here's a formula for determining just how large a set you will need to buy. Measure the distance from your chair to where the TV will be, multiply by 12, then divide by 3.

distance x 12, divided by three = minimum screen size**

**If the answer is larger than 40 inches, you will know that you will need a projection set. Remember that this formula is just a recommendation, not a rule. I for one like a larger set than the formula suggests.

Best Value Direct-View TV: Magnavox 27-inch Model No. PT2795C

$650

"Smart, Very Smart" is Magnavox's motto, and this 27-inch stereo TV is just that. At $650 it delivers a good picture and lots of bells and whistles at a very affordable price.

Included are convenience features such as smart sound, which automatically lowers those annoying, higher volume, blaring commercials that startle you out of your chair to a "normal" level. It also includes one of my favorite features: a remote control locator. When you can't find the remote, just go up to the television and press its power button. This triggers the remote to beep so you can figure out which couch cushion it is hiding under.

Other features include picture in picture (PIP) and instant replay with slow motion capability that plays back the last eight seconds of what you are watching in the PIP display.

Audiowise it incorporates two built-in speakers and includes a feature that simulates surround sound. Also included are a universal remote, audio/video inputs and outputs, and an S-video jack.

Best Direct-View TV: Sony KV-32XBR100

$3,300

This 32-inch set delivers a truly one of a kind picture quality—the good kind! Yes, it's fantastic, but unfortunately, at $3,300 you may opt to bypass purchasing it and decide to travel to one of those exotic locations seen on the Discovery Channel instead of watching a show about it.

Like many computers, this television has two parts: a monitor with Sony's finest Trinitron super-flat picture tube and a separate box (about the size of a VCR) that contains all the video circuitry, the tuner, and the necessary input and output connections.

Its high-end features include a digital comb filter for sharper pictures and an NTSC standard mode that lowers the color temperature to equal that used in professional video monitors (6500 Kelvin). Its remote features a unique joystick that utilizes an on-screen display to control all of your home theater's system components.

Other features include a built-in 44-watt amp with eight tiny speakers that are concealed around the monitor's exterior to give you the best sound possible. Five sets of A/V inputs, S-video connections, and outputs for an external sound system are also included. Because of its two-piece configuration, Sony was able to create a wedge-shaped chassis for the back of the TV, so when placing the set in a corner it takes up no more depth than a 20-inch television. It sells for $3,300—so I am yet again tempted to say *Show me the money!*

Best Wide-Screen TV: Toshiba TW40F80

$3,300

Although wide-screen televisions are not for everyone, for the video purist, it's the only way to go.

That's because wide-screen sets incorporate the preferred movie playback screen size: a rectangular 16:9 format as opposed to traditional, nearly square 4:3 aspect ratio screens.

Measuring 44⅝x37⅞x16 in., Toshiba's award-winning rear-screen projector is the first TV on the market with DVD component video hookups. Owners of DVD players are able to connect it directly to the set, allowing for much more accurate color and a very detailed picture.

Picture quality is what really makes this set shine. It features Toshiba's unique viewing modes (standard, theater wide, and full). This allows users to watch programs in the traditional style (with black bars displayed to the right and left of the picture to fill in the unused space) to theater wide (magically transforms a standard TV broadcast or movie to a wide-screen image) to full screen (fills the screen). A built-in digital comb filter and plenty of brightness, which can produce up to 800 lines of horizontal resolution, enhance all of these features.

Audiowise, the unit's base has a 14-watt amp and two 6-inch speakers. It comes with a remote control and sells for $3,300.

The good news about wide-screen sets is that they are ideal for viewing movies and for the new DVD players. The bad news is that when watching standard news and sports broadcasts, the graphics might be clipped off the top or the bottom of the screen. I have had one in my home for more than a year, and I have to say that once you get used to them, they are great—especially if you are watching movies. Its theater wide mode takes a standard image and with a little stretching and clipping comfortably converts it into a wide-screen image.

Before buying a wide-screen set, make sure to spend the time in the store playing with all its viewing modes. They are not for everyone.

Best Texas-Sized TV: ProScan PS80690 80-inch Projection TV

$8,500

If *big* is your middle name, then the ProScan 80-inch is the best set for you.

This behemoth upgrades standard 7-inch projection tubes by replacing them with giant 9-inch models that deliver a 50 percent brighter picture with a whopping 800 lines of horizontal resolution. It has a digital comb filter, digital video noise reduction, an adjustable color temperature, and get this: its PIP is the same size as a 35-inch television's.

Its channel guide allows you to monitor up to twelve programs at the same time—so you'll never miss what's going on. And its split screen allows you to watch two programs simultaneously and hear one through its speakers and the other via headphones. This way the adults and youngsters can spend an entertaining evening in the same room.

Its audio is as big as its video and includes an on-screen graphic equalizer, a 55-watt Dolby Pro Logic amplifier, a center channel speaker, and front enclosure speaker system.

Despite the fact that you may have to add on to your house, this set is relatively trim and only 36 inches deep, but it stands almost 10 inches taller than either John or myself, measuring 75⅛x69⅜ in., and weighing a mere 650 pounds. The good news is that you'll probably never have to dust its top—unless Shaquille O'Neal is coming over for dinner. It has 31 gold-plated jack inputs and outputs at the rear.

The only thing bigger than this set is the hole it will leave in your wallet. Did I mention it sells for $8,500? But hey, John and I both agree that if we got one next to the menorah or under the tree, we would reread *The Gadget Guru's Make-It-Easy Guide to Home Repair* (okay, a shameless plug) to figure out how to make it fit into our respective homes.

Best TV for Your Kitchen: RCA KitchenVision Model No. T13070WH

$480

The best way to learn to cook is to watch somebody else do it. That's the idea behind the KitchenVision, a combination 13-inch color TV with a built-in VCR.

Measuring just 15¾x14½x15 in., this kitchen-white TV/VCR features a built-in swivel base and earphone jack. Its unique remote control has a no-spill, wipe clean protective cover that promises to keep your secret spaghetti sauce off the electronics.

Its two-head VCR features an eight-event/one-year programmable timer, auto head-cleaner, and best of all it comes with an Italian cooking video titled *The de Medici Kitchen,* featuring numerous recipes to help get you started cooking in no time. Or you can make your own video. Just take a camcorder over to your favorite chef's home (my sister-in-law

Maria's), videotape her cooking technique, and play it back to duplicate the recipe.

Best Handheld TV: Sony Color Watchman Model No. FDL-22

$130

Those of us on the go who don't want to miss a minute of the action should check out this new handheld model from Sony.

Called the Watchman with straptenna, this tiny TV set features a 2.2-inch color LCD screen and unique antenna that is concealed inside the unit's neck strap.

Because the strap is worn around your neck, it uses your body as a kind of signal booster—meaning the unit will have better reception, whether you're picnicking in the parking lot, watching the game from the stands, or tanning on the beach.

It measures just 6⅛x3¼x1¾ in.

Best TV for Your Bedroom: Mitsubishi CV-20125 TV/VCR

$600

There are two reasons I am not a big fan of combination TV/VCRs. First, if something breaks on the VCR and you have to take it in for repair, you are sans a TV. Second, combination models contain only one tuner, so unlike a separate television and VCR you cannot record one show while watching another.

Forgetting my reservations, a combination TV/VCR for the bedroom or a secondary room makes perfect sense. The good news is that by combining both of these components in a tidy package, space is saved. Also, since the VCR is incorporated into the television, no wiring is required.

Mitsubishi's 20-inch unit combines an excellent color picture with a four-head VCR. This model is not stereo, so if you plan on watching a lot of movies you may want to upgrade to a stereo TV/VCR unit. Mitsubishi's VCR does allow for the recording of up to five separate events over a one-month period. When you consider that you are getting two products in one, its $600 price tag sounds affordable.

Other features include front panel jacks for camcorders or video game systems, a 181 channel tuner, an on-screen clock, and an automatic head-cleaner, plus one of my favorites: a childproof lock on the VCR loading door that keeps the little one's peanut butter and jelly out of your electronics. It includes a remote control that operates both the VCR and TV.

TV GADGETS AND ACCESSORIES

Best Use of a TV, or Best Product for Jetson Wannabes: 8X8 Via TV

$500

Video telephones have become a reality.

Like those seen in

the old Jetsons cartoons, videophones are designed to allow telephone callers to not only speak to those on the other end of the line, but see them as well.

For those not in the know, video telephones are small, unobtrusive electronic boxes that are designed to rest atop a television set. They include a tiny color camera and a 33.6 kbps (kilobits per second) speed modem and connect to a telephone line, a power outlet, and the television. Both the audio and video portions of the call are transmitted to and from the recipient over a standard phone line.

To make a videophone call you simply place yourself in front of the camera, call the desired phone number, wait for the party to answer, and agree to "go video" with the call. Within a few seconds the other person's image magically appears on your television and vice versa.

Of course, both parties on the call must have a video telephone to partake in this experience. The good news is that although there are a number of competing companies getting into this arena, most of the videophones currently on the market are compatible. They also are capable of communicating with many of the video telephones designed for use with computers.

The other bit of good news is that it costs no more to make a videophone call than it does to make a standard phone call.

The bad news is that the video quality is not up to par with the images we are used to seeing on our televisions. That's because only 4 to 15 frames per second of video appear on the screen during a video telephone call (as opposed to the 30 frames per second delivered by broadcast television). This rate is determined by the quality of the telephone line connection and the specific settings on each unit. Although the sound is delivered in real time, the video image is strobelike. It takes a while to get used to the sound not matching the lips of the person talking.

Videophones are ideal for those who desire visual contact with friends and loved ones who reside in another city, or for grandparents to keep an eye on their grandchildren. They are also an inexpensive and effective method of videoconferencing for businesses.

Best On-Screen TV Guide: StarSight

$3.50 per month

```
           S T A R S I G H T
SEP    MON TUE WED THU FRI SAT SUN
 7        8:00P           8:30P
CSP2   News1          U.S.Senate
CNN    Primenews
 26    Mathnet: Despair in Monter
SHOW   City Slickers
HBO    Bingo
DISC   All in a Day's Work
ESPN   Major League Baseball (L)
FAM    Batman
 4     Fresh Prince │ Blossom
DISN   Avonlea
SHOW   SHOWTIME CBL 37       7:30P
```

Because this product is found on TVs, VCRs, and satellite receivers, it is difficult to categorize under just one subject heading. Nonetheless, if you are serious about TV and VCR recording or looking for the easiest method of navigating the seemingly endless assortment of TV channels, StarSight is the best on-screen TV listing guide on the planet.

StarSight is a subscription-based interactive on-screen television guide that delivers up-to-date listings of television programs. Unlike listing services carried by cable companies, StarSight delivers a week's worth of shows, gives you program descriptions, and even sets your VCR to record a television show at the press of a button.

And best of all, it is simple to use.

Once StarSight is connected to your television, you just press the remote control's guide button and up comes a multicolored, on-screen television grid that displays the names and times of the programs on the first ten channels of your cable lineup for the next 90 minutes. To see more channels, you just press the arrow or page keys. When you want more information on a specific show, you just use the remote arrows to highlight the desired program and press its star button to view a description of the show, leading cast members, the duration, episode details, and, if it's a movie, the rating and release year.

Now here's the fun part: If you want to record that show, you just push the record button. Another screen is displayed that asks if you want to record it once, weekly, or daily. All you have to remember to do is place a tape in the VCR. I have to say that this is the simplest method ever of recording on your VCR.

The StarSight theme button allows you to find a program by category. Once pressed, it displays a list of eight categories ranging from specials and children's programming to news, sports, and entertainment. Highlighting the desired category produces a list of current and upcoming programs. To change the channel to the selected program, you just press the tune button and it jumps to the proper channel.

Movies can be chosen in the same manner. Just select one of the ten themes, peruse through a list, and tune it in or record it—all with the press of a few easy-to-use buttons.

Of all the products I have reviewed over the years, few have impressed me as much as StarSight. As our cable systems grow to include more than 100 channels, this promises to be the best method introduced to date of finding and recording television programs. StarSight is available on more than a dozen consumer electronics companies' products including TVs, VCRs, and satellite receivers. A service fee of $3.50 per month will provide all the listings.

Best Value Remote Control: Universal Director 8

$50

These days, almost every piece of new electronic equipment includes a remote control. So, for many of us, our coffee tables are nothing more than a place to rest them all.

That's where universal remote controls come into play. These units can consolidate numerous remote controls into one easy-to-use unit.

Our best value remote control is Universal's A/V Director 8—a sleekly styled remote that includes the right buttons to operate up to eight different pieces of electronic equipment, including the new small satellite dishes and DVD players.

The remote has preprogrammed infrared codes for more than 300 of the most popular audio, video, cable boxes, and satellite brands.

Other features include a home theater mode key, which allows you to customize your home theater audio and video, PIP controls, and a TV/DSS key to help users toggle between satellite and TV signals—which is especially helpful for the viewing of local stations. It has a backlit keypad and an LCD screen that displays information about the functions in use, and timed macros for programming advanced preset functions like VCR recordings.

Best Remote Control: Marantz RC2000

$250

If you're serious about home theater, the Marantz RC2000 is the ultimate remote control for managing your audio and video needs.

Although it looks like a high-tech device found on the Starship *Enterprise,* this unit is not only relatively simple to set up, it is also easy to operate and incorporates functions that were previously found on models costing hundreds of dollars more than its $250 price tag.

No, it's not cheap—but it is the only remote control I have found that can fully operate extensive home theater systems.

Unlike other remotes, this model can learn the necessary codes to almost any remote ever made. It accomplishes this feat by reading the code from the dedicated remote control and storing it in its memory.

The RC2000 can control up to ten different components at one time, ranging from TVs, VCRs, and digital satellite systems to CD players and receivers. In fact, I personally tried to stump it by teaching it codes from remotes that other remotes refused to accept and it passed with flying colors

It is 8½x3⅛x1½ in., and ergonomically designed to fit comfortably in your hand. It features a large backlit LCD window and keys that make it simple to find the right button even in a dark room. Simply press any key or side-mounted button and both the keypad and LCD monitor are illuminated.

For automation purposes, it includes four macro keys, which can transmit up to 20 commands at the touch of a button. Each macro key can be programmed to activate your entire home theater system, adjust the surround sound, and even start a movie—in any order you choose.

Four AA batteries power it and the only drawback is that the batteries need to be replaced about every 45 days.

Best Wireless TV Device: RF-Link WaveComSr

$250

Wireless transmitters can be the answer if you want to avoid purchasing an additional VCR, DVD player, satellite receiver, or just about any piece of audio/video equipment.

Our favorite wireless transmitter on the market today is the WaveComSr. This model is capable of sending video and stereo audio signals from one unit to another (up to 300 feet away) and through walls, ceilings and floors. This allows you to not only control the devices, but watch cable, VCR, or satellite programs on your bedroom TV without a separate hookup, or movies in a bedroom without moving the VCR or laser disc player from the family room. You can even hook it up to your camcorder and TV and monitor your baby.

Signals are transmitted via an FM signal at 2.4 GHz, as opposed to other wireless products, which use a lower 900 MHz frequency that can often conflict with cordless phones or other wireless devices. One feature I really like is its built-in remote control extender that allows you to change the channel, adjust the volume, or control your equipment from one room to another with the unit's existing remote. This works by converting the remote control's infrared signals to radio waves and then back into infrared at the equipment to be controlled. All this happens instantaneously, without any effort on your part.

Best Television Remote to Make Coffee with: RCA Home Director

$60

Couch potatoes will surely love this product—a remote control that will allow them to take command of a television, VCR, cable box, lights, even a coffeemaker all from the comfort of his or her easy chair.

It is called the Home Director and it utilizes small modules to control just about any electrically powered device in the home. Included in the

kit are a base module and a remote control. The base module plugs into the wall and just about any electrical appliance can be plugged into it. Up to 15 modules or switches can be placed around the house. The modules are activated by the included UHF remote control. Each module has a specific code number. A lamp could be number 3 and the coffeemaker number 8. To operate, just press the remote's home button, the corresponding module number, and "on." This sends a radio signal to the base, which then sends a signal through your home's existing electrical wiring system that tells that module to provide power to the unit. Even better, if the module is connected to a lamp, a press of a button commands it to dim or brighten. This same remote control also operates your television, VCR, and cable box. The only restriction to its operation is that the remote has to be within 75 feet of the base module—but since the signal is UHF the base module can be located behind a wall or in another room.

To add more appliances, just install a separate module and assign them a number. Additional extensions can be purchased for about $17.

Best TV Product for the Truly Lazy: Telectra TI 3000

$200

Imagine that you are sitting on the couch watching television when the phone rings. Instead of having to walk all the way over to the caller ID box to see the name and number of the person calling, you simply look at your television, where this information is automatically superimposed over the program you are watching.

Yes, it doesn't get any easier than this. The Telectra TI 3000 is an 8x6x3 in. device that displays caller ID/name ID information on your television screen. It connects to a television, VCR, or cable box and a telephone line to bring this information to the big screen.

When a call comes in, it displays the caller's name, phone number, and the date and time of the call in the lower left-hand corner of the television screen. Of course, you have to subscribe to the phone company's caller ID service for this product to operate properly. And you still have to get up and go to the bathroom every once in a while too.

Best Weapon against Channel Surfers: The Remote Blocker

$20

Everybody knows one person that has the annoying habit of trying to watch multiple television shows simultaneously. These folks are called channel surfers, and if you've ever tried to enjoy watching a program with a surfer, you know that at the least it is frustrating, if not impossible.

Well, now there's a product that can give you power over the surfer. It's The Remote Blocker and with a press of a button it sends an infrared signal that blocks the surfer's remote control and renders it basically useless. To use, just aim The Remote Blocker at the surfer when he or she is trying to use the remote control to change channels. Then press the button. This will make it impossible for him or her to change channels—meaning that you can sit back and relax while the culprit is trying to figure out what's wrong.

It features an LED lamp that indicates a blocked signal is being transmitted, rendering your channel surfer helpless and pleading for mercy. It sells for $20. It is also available in a key chain size for $10.

VCRs

Let's face it, the VCR has changed our lives. We no longer have to adjust our schedules to watch a favorite television program; we can record it and watch it at our leisure. Or, if there's nothing on TV, we can head out to the video store and peruse the more than 10,000 movie titles for entertainment.

This year's new VCRs offer even more convenience features such as one-button recording, options that eliminate commercials upon playback, and a hot new feature that eliminates the promotional coming attractions commonly included on movie rentals.

There are two types of VCRs:

S-VHS VCRs: High-end VCRs that deliver up to 400 lines of resolution. S-VHS machines are best for the video purist and video editors—those who shoot and edit a lot of camcorder footage. They have more editing features on them. And of course they cost a lot more.

VHS VCRs: These VCRs deliver up to 240 lines of video resolution and come in two-, four-, and six-head models. Audiowise there are hi-fi and analog. VHS VCRs are the most common.

   Buying Tip: For your primary VCR, look for hi-fi units with at least four video heads. For a secondary room a two-head VCR will do just fine.

VCR GLOSSARY

Auto clock set: Yes, everyone from Carson to Seinfeld to Letterman paid the rent with jokes about the flashing 12:00 syndrome in the '80s. However, almost all VCRs today come with auto clock set that automatically sets the VCR clock through a signal broadcast from PBS stations. Auto clock set probably ended some comedians' careers.

Auto head-cleaner: Another nice feature. Eliminates the need for messy liquid cleaner accessories. Great for excessive usage—especially for those parents who've seen the *Lion King* 3,000 times.

Child lock: Speaking of parents, many VCRs come with this feature that keeps your child's curious fingers out of your electronics by locking the tape door when not in use.

Flying erase heads: Sounds like a circus act, but it's actually an advanced editing feature for the camcorder-to-VCR editing enthusiast. A great feature for the recording crowd, but not necessary for most users.

Jog shuttle dial: More goofy jargon. Jog shuttle just allows you to speed up your fast forward/reverse on the VCR. Once again, a good feature for editing.

Programmable timer: If you do a lot of recording make sure your VCR has at least an eight-event/one-year timer so you don't have to set the thing all the time. Also look for units that have StarSight (see page 18). This subscription service for $3.50 a month allows for one-touch VCR recording.

VCR Plus+: A recording aid that allows you to enter numbers from printed TV listing for easy one-step recording.

Best No-Frills Value VCR: Samsung VR8806

$329

If you're an average VCR user—someone who records a few shows and rents a few movies every so often, there's  really no need to go out and purchase a VCR with every bell and whistle known to man. What you need is a good, low-cost dependable unit.

Samsung's VR8806 is just the ticket. Featuring four video heads and hi-fi audio, this VCR delivers all the necessary features of more expensive VCRs at a very affordable price tag: $329.

It includes an automatic clock set feature and a preprogrammed remote control with an oversized dial for easy fast-forwarding/rewinding. The remote also controls most televisions and has an infrared device that sits atop your cable box and allows you to change cable channels as well. Other features include an eight-event/one-year programmable timer and some advanced viewing options like multispeed fast-forward and reverse, slow motion viewing, freeze-frame, and frame advance.

Best Step-Up VCR: Toshiba M-782

$600

Although introduced last year, this VCR continues to set the benchmark for quality in the mid-price range.

Featuring a six-head mechanism that delivers one of the highest-quality video images I've ever seen (due in part to a new digital noise-reduction circuit, which enhances the quality of older, somewhat worn videotapes), this Toshiba VCR is definitely a technological wonder.

Other features include hi-fi audio, VCR Plus+, and an eight-event/one-year programmable timer as well as its super-fast rewind that makes it easy to "be kind and rewind" rental movies. It comes with a pre-programmed remote control with keys for slow motion and frame by frame advancement.

Best New Feature on a VCR: RCA Model No. VR654HF with Movie Advance

$350

As consumers we are all victims of advertising in our daily life. Whether it's on television, radio, the Internet, or displayed on billboards

scattered along the side of the road, no public forum is sacred. Even the videotapes we rent are now filled with movie previews, advertisements, and other promotions that we must suffer through even though we have paid good money to rent or purchase the movie. Combating this problem is RCA's latest VCR feature called movie advance. This technology automatically skips over those annoying movie previews found on video rentals.

Like its companion feature commercial advance, which automatically fast-forwards through commercials on your prerecorded television programs, movie advance allows you to press a button on the VCR's remote and watch as those time-consuming and boring movie previews and commercials whiz by at lightning speed. Here's how it works: Simply insert the rental tape and press the movie advance key on the remote control. It then, by some mysterious mathematical method, knows when the ads start and end and magically fast-forwards to the beginning of the movie. Once movie advance locates the beginning of the movie, it pauses the tape and informs you that it is ready to play. During that time, so that you don't get a headache looking at the fast-forward scanning, a pleasant blue screen is displayed.

Other features include an auto clock set, an eight-event/one-year programmable timer, plus a universal remote control with basic functions for up to 30 brands of televisions, cable boxes, or various RCA satellite receivers (DSS).

Best Dual Deck VCR: Go-Video Encore GV6600

$800

Dual deck VCRs are the Rodney Dangerfields of the electronics industry—they get no respect.

But for those of us who need to periodically

make copies of our family videos they can be a lifesaver. These units enclose two tape mechanisms in one nice, tidy, albeit larger than normal size unit. Although you can accomplish this task by connecting two VCRs together, dual deck VCRs eliminate the wiring mess and make it simple for even the technologically impaired to dub the images from one tape to another.

Go-Video is the company that bucked the powers that be by introducing the first dual deck unit earlier this decade. It has since become the leader in the two-in-one industry and earned the reputation of delivering good-quality, innovative dual deck VCRs.

This model features a new design that stacks the individual decks on top of each other as opposed to stretching the two decks side by side, thereby reducing the cabinet space needed to house the VCR.

The Encore is only 7⅜x14⅜ in., and although about twice as tall as most VCRs, features the same footprint of standard VCRs so it can rest in the same cabinet as the audio receiver, CD player, or satellite receiver.

It works like this: With a simple push of a button, both the videotapes are rewound. One deck plays the tape and the other records. After the copy is made, it automatically rewinds both tapes.

Other features include four video heads, hi-fi stereo circuitry, and although there is only one tuner, there are separate audio/video inputs on each deck that, depending on your setup, allows for two programs to be recorded simultaneously. Or, if multiple copies are needed, both decks can be set to record the same program.

Ultimate VCR: JVC HRS 9400U S-VHS

$1,200

If you're serious about video editing or just want about the best picture available from a VCR, this unit from JVC takes the cake.

This model features four video heads, hi-fi stereo audio, and delivers more than 400 lines of horizontal resolution for the best picture playback capability on a consumer VCR today.

Its video circuitry includes three tiny computer chips, which contain a comb filter for better color, digital noise reduction, and a feature called dynamic contrast control, which at the touch of a button improves contrast, sharpness, and detail.

For home movie enthusiasts the VCR's advanced editing features include flying erase heads for smoother transitions between recordings, audio dubbing for adding background music to your home movies, and jog shuttle dials on both the unit and remote control for faster scene-searching.

Other features include an eight-event/one-year programmable timer, commercial advance, VCR Plus+ program guide for recording, and a multibrand illuminated remote control with an instant review button that automatically finds and plays back a previously recorded program at the press of a button.

CAMCORDERS

Whether it's baby's first steps, Grandma's eightieth birthday, or your little girl's first dance recital, the camcorder has become the best method ever of recording and sharing your family's memories. But choosing the right camcorder for your lifestyle can be a difficult task. The first decision a new buyer has to make is which format to purchase. There are currently four different formats that spawn seven somewhat confusing choices, so you should consider your needs and options carefully.

VHS CAMCORDERS

Pros: Least expensive. Uses standard VHS tapes that pop out of the camcorder and into a VHS VCR without the use of adapters or confusing wire connections.

Cons: Because of the tape size, VHS camcorders are larger, more cumbersome, and heavier than their compact counterparts. Although not a bad choice if it is going to be used around the house, not my pick for trying to record memories while on vacation.

SUPER-VHS

Pros: Higher resolution than VHS, more editing features.

Cons: Same as above.

VHS-C CAMCORDERS

Pros: Although the tape itself is the same width as VHS, it is housed in a smaller, much more compact cassette. This allows VHS-C camcorders to be smaller and lighter. Instead of having to connect wires to play back (see 8 mm below), all VHS-C camcorders include an adapter that is the same size as a VHS tape and allows for easy playback on any VCR.

Cons: The cassettes only allow up to 40 minutes of recording time in the standard, high-quality mode.

SUPER VHS-C

Pros: Same as VHS-C, but it records and plays back a much higher-quality image and hi-fi audio.

Cons: Same as above.

8-MM CAMCORDERS

Pros: Uses a videocassette about the same size as an audiocassette and delivers up to two hours of recording. Like VHS-C, the smaller tape results in smaller, lighter camcorders.

Cons: 8-MM tapes do not play in VHS VCRs. To play back, the camcorder needs a hard wire connection to a VCR or television.

This means that your camcorder acts not only as a recording mechanism, but a playback deck as well. This results in additional wear and tear on the camcorder.

HI8

Pros: Same as 8 mm, but it records and plays back a much higher-quality image and hi-fi audio.

Cons: Same as above.

DIGITAL CAMCORDERS, OR DVC

Pros: As close to true professional video as you can get at home. The DVC format delivers 500 lines of horizontal resolution, as opposed to the 400 lines of S-VHS-C and Hi8 formats and the 240 lines provided by VHS and 8 mm. It provides the best pictures and ultimate editing capabilities of both TVs and computers. The computer applications range from printing out still images to uploading and transferring them to another computer. DVCs are very small and lightweight.

Cons: Expensive, $2600+. Not compatible with all video systems.

Best Value Camcorder: RCA Model No. CC641 VHS-C Camcorder

$550

For the best no-frills camcorder on the market, this VHS-C camcorder leaves plenty of dough left over for the family vacation.

It features an 18:1 optical zoom lens, auto focus, built-in lens cover, and a select

number of special effects such as fading and wiping in to and out of specific scenes. It measures 8½x4½x4½ in. and weights just 1.8 pounds with battery. Other features include an automatic head-cleaner and a dew sensor that protects the video heads.

Best View Screen Camcorder: Sharp VL-E750U

$1,100

Sharp was the first camcorder manufacturer to incorporate an LCD screen into camcorders. This innovative feature allows for not only an oversized viewfinder that eliminates the squinting associated with using these devices, but also grants immediate playback and group viewing of your movies.

This model features an extra-large 4-inch color LCD screen incorporated on the back of this unit that all but eliminates the need to connect it to a television to view your footage.

Other features include a 12:1 optical zoom and 32:1 digital zoom, digital image stabilization that takes the shake out of movies, automatic brightness controls for crisper pictures, and digital effects including still, snapshot strobe, and fade. Its viewfinder rotates 180 degrees for self-recording, and also has variable angle recording that allows for cinema-like angle shots for more creative home videos.

It includes a 90-minute battery and measures 4³⁹⁄₆₄x7³¹⁄₆₄x3²⁵⁄₃₂ in. and weighs 1.79 pounds without the battery.

Best Feature on a Camcorder: Canon ES6000 with Optical Image Stabilization

$1,700

This Hi8 camcorder features one of the least understood but best technologies found on any camcorder: optical image stabilization.

Optical image stabilization (OIS) is superior to electronic image stabilization (EIS) found on many high-end camcorders. While both systems relieve the shaky hand syndrome, EIS does so at the expense of picture quality. Optical image stabilization provides for shake-free filming without any degradation of picture quality by incorporating Canon's proprietary technology called Vari-Angle prism.

Another unique feature is its eye control focus. Instead of relying on the camcorder's internal circuitry to focus on the center part of the subject or image, this camcorder divides the lens into segments and focuses on the image you are looking at. This is ideal when shooting a subject that is standing in front of a house or other large background. Instead of the background being in focus, it will focus on the subject—as long as you are looking directly at it. This eye-calibration feature can also be used to activate and control a variety of switches, including start and stop recording, digital effects, fades, and wipes.

The first time you use the camcorder it calibrates your eye's movement in a simple ten-second procedure that uses infrared beams to record your individual eye's focus patterns. Once the camera is calibrated (it can store the readings for up to three different users), just look through the viewfinder and direct your eye to any subject in the frame—the camcorder will automatically focus in that direction. When you look elsewhere in the frame, the unit immediately refocuses on that area. The results are terrific because the camera actually focuses on the exact subject you want to record.

As mentioned, it also allows you to control other functions such as start and stop recording, digital effects, fades, and wipes by simply looking at its eye-controlled menu also housed inside the viewfinder.

Other features include a color LCD viewfinder lens, a 20:1 optical zoom lens and a 40:1 digital zoom lens, hi-fi stereo, and built-in auto editing features that enable you to edit easily between the camcorder and a VCR without the use of separate editing devices. It delivers 420 lines of horizontal resolution, and it has a manual control option as well.

Best Video Camera for Kids: Tyco VideoCam

$100

If you've got a budding Spielberg or Coppola running around the house, then you may want to check out the new VideoCam from Tyco.

The reason that it costs less than a camcorder is that it does not include the recording mechanism. To record, you connect it to any standard VCR—the cable is included.

It features an easy-to-use one-button control and operates on 6 AA batteries. There are no complicated manuals or focusing procedures. Parents simply make a one-time connection with an included 23-foot cable that is tethered between the VCR's audio/video inputs and the camcorder. Images and sounds can be recorded on a VCR tape or viewed live on TV.

Weighing just 15 ounces, it's perfect for even the tiniest director, and with its fixed focus lens and automatic light adjustment, filming is a snap. Although it is not designed to bounce on hard floors, it most likely will survive reasonable abuse. The VideoCam is designed for children ages six and up. It comes with a camera storage bag, tripod, and an additional set of quick-connect audio/video cables. A color VideoCam may be available by the end of the year and sell for $150.

Best Digital Camcorder (Tie): JVC GR-DVM1 and Sony DCRVX700

Both under $3,000

For the best consumer digital camera it's a toss-up between JVC's GR-DVM1 and Sony's DCRVX700.

Both models use the new mini DVC (digital video cassette), which, at a mere 2x2½x¼ in., delivers up to 60 minutes of digital recording on a single cassette.

Since the tape is so small, the camcorders can be designed to be compact. The Sony model measures only 5⅛x4⅝x2⅜ in. and weighs 1½ pounds with the battery. The JVC unit measures 6⅛x3¾x3⅜ in. and weighs 1.8 pounds with the battery.

Both units also include LCD screens that can be used as viewfinders or playback monitors. The screens rotate 270 degrees for full, multi-angle viewing and fold flat when not in use.

Although you can transfer digital movies from these camcorders to your VCR, because of the resolution limitations of a VCR (400 lines versus 500 lines digital), the picture quality will not be as good as the tape. For seamless editing and playback, Sony has a mini DVC VCR that connects to digital camcorders. Although the JVC will work on the Sony DVC VCR, JVC is also offering an optional docking station ($340) that provides easy hookup to a computer for digital editing.

The bottom line is that you can't go wrong with either model.

CD PLAYERS

Some products are evolutionary; others are revolutionary. The compact disk (CD) falls into the latter category.

When CD players were first introduced in the early 1980s, they were viewed as being not only a technological breakthrough but also as the logical replacement for the phonograph record. Unlike other attempted format launches whose attributes had to be explained to potential purchasers, the benefits of the CD were immediately obvious. First of all, they're smaller—only 5 inches in diameter versus the LP's 12-inch size— they're resistant to scratches, and they deliver a sound that makes even moderate stereo systems much better. Even more important, because there is no physical contact between the pickup lens and the disc, CDs do not show wear and tear.

Although initial CD players held $1,000 price tags, they flew off retailers' shelves. In fact, even at that price they were hard to find.

Nowadays, things are different. For around $100 you can find a single-disc player that includes more features than the original $1,000 models. But that's not where the action is. Today, retail activity is flourishing around models that store and play a drawerful of these shiny silver-colored marvels. To simplify your search, here are our picks for the best of the year.

Best Value Multiple-Disc CD Player: Fisher Studio 60 Model No. DAC 6006

$300

Once you insert a CD in this unit, you may never need to see it or touch it again. That's because this model stores up to 60 CDs and allows you to assign them to a number of categories that makes playing back music for specific occasions a press-of-a-button experience.

It features a CD management system that allows you to assign each disc to custom categories such as musical type (jazz, rock, classical), moods (morning, romantic, rainy day), family member (Mom's picks, Dad's favorites), occasion (birthdays, anniversaries, parties), or by performer (Sting, Doobie Brothers, Tony Bennett).

Its remote control allows you to select the category and playback functions as well as program the unit's built-in scrolling digital display from the comfort of your easy chair.

Other features include an optical digital output for connection to any amplifier or digital-to-analog converter, and a dust-free storage chamber, which protects your CD library and the internal mechanisms. Although taller than single-disc models, it can still fit into most furniture components. It is 7¼x16½x17½ in.

Best High-End CD Changer: Marantz CC-65SE

$500

True audio aficionados prefer single-disc models that can cost upwards of $1,000. But today, many high-end manufacturers are creating multiple-disc changers that meet the demands of the discerning audiophile. And let's face it, multiple-disc players are the ultimate convenience item allowing for hours of uninterrupted music.

The Marantz five-disc CD changer is packed with high-end features like a fader control and a peak-search button, which allows you to set your cassette recording levels perfectly each time. It has a coaxial digital output and lots of buttons on the front of the unit for multiple-disc shuffle play, and random modes. Other features include a carousel that will play a selected CD while allowing you to load the other four discs, and a unique two-sided remote control with buttons for the CD changer on the front side and other components on the back.

Best CD Behemoth: Sony Model No. CDP-CX90ES 200-Disc Changer

$1,100

With internal storage for up to 200 compact discs, this CD changer from Sony can store drawers full of CDs.

This unit has a unique keyboard port on the back that connects to any Windows-based computer keyboard. This allows for easy and convenient entry of disc and track titles for organizing your music according to themes (jazz, rock, classical) or customized listening options for that hot date on Saturday night. It includes a custom file system with eight different group categories, a remote control with a jog shuttle dial for quick scrolling through disc titles, and a 10-key direct access track, group, and disc selection.

The CD unit features a large backlit screen, which displays disc and track titles, a shuttle dial for quick selection, and an easy-load bay. Its back panel has A/V inputs and two AC outputs as well. Even better, if you own more than 200 CDs, the unit can be daisy chained with a second Sony 200-disc player and all 400 titles controlled via the same remote.

Despite its capacity the unit will fit in most A/V cabinetry. It measures 7⅜x17x19 in.

Best Designed CD Jukebox: JVC XL-MC302

$870

CD changers are traditionally over-sized CD players that not only play back your CDs but store them as well.

This model from JVC bucks the tradition of having to cram one of the oversized units in your bookshelf or stereo rack by separating them into two components. The first is a standard-sized single-disc CD player that con-

trols a second component—a 14¾₆x14⅞₆x14¹³₆ in. 100-disc CD storage unit that can be placed out of sight and away from your other components.

Although separated, a cable connects the two components, which are controlled by electronics incorporated in the single-disc player. Users can access titles from the 100-disc storage cube or simply load a CD in the controller's tray. Its user file function allows you to create 10 files (i.e. music type, artist) that hold up to 32 discs each in its memory. Its delete file key allows you to remove unwanted tracks as well, while its remote control includes an LCD screen, which displays disc titles, file names, and has an index search for scrolling through your collection.

Like the aforementioned product, the JVC 100-disc storage unit can be daisy chained with up to two additional 100-disc units for a total of 300-disc storage—all controlled via a single remote.

A bonus good-thinking award also goes to JVC for including a CD booklet file with 100 slots for easy organization. This way, you can assemble your own catalog of titles and flip through them at your leisure. Additional changers sell for $550.

STEREOS

Back in 1979 I had my first experience with a portable stereo. I was working for Panasonic and we had just received these small, albeit not pocket-sized, battery-operated tape machines that instead of speakers, included a pair of headphones.

I had taken this unit on an airplane to see how practical they would be in real-life situations. As luck would have it, I was seated just behind the airplane's wing—and was exposed to the deafening engine sounds. I took the unit out of my briefcase, popped in a tape, and put on the headphones. *Wow!* This was outrageous. Not only did it drown out the engine sounds, the quality of the audio coming out of this tiny box was amazing. The tape sounded better with this machine than it did in my home or car stereo systems.

When I got back to the office and was talking to my co-workers about my experience with this product, everyone agreed that these things were absolutely amazing. The only question the sales staff had was "Would it sell?"

Although we did not have the answer then, I can look back now and say a resounding *yes!*

But it took the marketing expertise of Sony to make it happen.

Most may not remember, but about that same time Sony introduced its first portable stereo system and called it the Soundabout. About a year or so later, Sony changed the name to the Walkman. We all thought that the powers that be at Sony had lost their marbles—what a strange name.

Today, although the name "Walkman" belongs to Sony, it is synonymous with the category of portable stereos. Needless to say, not only have they become a big hit, it's hard to find someone who has never owned one.

While these tiny marvels are continuing to evolve with more features, longer battery life, and unique designs, the audio business is much deeper than portable stereos. There are boom boxes that can act as portable entertainment centers, mini systems that are ideal for the bookshelf or office, and powerful home systems that deliver great sounds and features at a reasonable cost.

But the biggest news these days in the audio industry is home theater.

Having spawned from the initial stereo televisions and VCRs, home theater systems have leaped ahead by allowing those at home to create an audio system that makes watching television or a movie a true theater-at-home experience.

The biggest home theater development of the decade is Dolby Pro Logic surround sound. This technology takes a stereo system and adds sophisticated electronic circuitry that allows movie dialogue to be isolated to a center channel speaker that is placed either directly above or below the television. The music comes from the left and right speakers and the special effects come from two rear speakers placed behind the viewer. The addition of a subwoofer to a Dolby Pro Logic system allows for the delivery of the deep bass sound that brings realism to movies at home.

Today, though, there is a new technology that brings movie theater sound one step closer to home. It's called Dolby Digital (a step up from Pro Logic) and what makes it different is that it separates the channels even more than its predecessors. Here's how it works: The voices still come from the center and the music comes from the left and right speakers. But instead of the rear speakers delivering the same effects, they are separate signals. This way, an airplane can sound as though it were flying overhead and crisscrossing a room just like in a theater. Also, the subwoofer will have a dedicated channel for more realistic bass effects.

The only bad news about Dolby Digital is that it requires the purchase of a new receiver or component(s), and dedicated software that is encoded with the Dolby Digital signal. Compared with Dolby Pro Logic, which can be used with basically any stereo signal, this makes Dolby Digital not as versatile. But allow me to add that just about every DVD movie will be encoded with this new technology. So if you are in the market for a DVD, the next step will most likely be a Dolby Digital system.

Needless to say, choosing the best audio products of the year was a difficult task.

Best Boom Box: Panasonic Model RX-ED77

$330

Although no audio manufacturer officially sanctions the term "boom box," I can think of no better way to describe these tote-along, big-speaker portable sound systems. This model from Panasonic not only sounds good, it looks great too!

It features an AM/FM tuner, a single-disc CD player, and dual-cassette deck. This space-age-looking portable stereo incorporates two 4-inch full-range speakers that deliver big sound. These speakers are mounted horizontally, as opposed to vertically, for better room-filling sound dispersion.

Just the touch of a remote control or front panel button instructs the mechanically operated control panel to magically appear and reveal an LCD panel, operating buttons, and the two tape compartments. It offers a one-touch CD-to-cassette recording technique with a unique CD synchro start button, which automatically begins CD play when the cassette deck's record button is pressed.

Other features include preset equalizer settings that allow users to choose the best sound for the music being played, a robust deep bass system, and enhanced mid-range frequencies for a wider sound.

It operates on 10 D batteries or with an included AC adapter.

Best Portable Cassette Player: Sony Anniversary Walkman

$300

In 1946 Harry Truman was president and Sony Electronics began operation. But it wasn't until Jimmy Carter's waning days (1979) that Sony introduced its revolutionary Walkman (then called the Soundabout) personal stereo. To celebrate its fifty years in business, Sony has introduced a specially designed Anniversary Walkman cassette player that is loaded with both style and substance.

What makes this model noteworthy is its sleek, mirrored-finish exterior and revolutionary 60-hour battery life. This feat is accomplished with the inclusion of two batteries—one a single AA alkaline and the other a rechargeable cell. The single AA battery will power the cassette mechanism for approximately 40 hours. By inserting its rechargeable cell, another 20 hours is added to its playback time.

Other features include a tiny but functional 1-inch square LCD on the headphone cord for easy operation of the cassette's fast-forward, reverse, play, and volume controls.

Best Portable CD Player: Panasonic ShockWave Model No. SL-SW405

$200

Characteristically, portable CD players have two problems: They skip when jarred or shaken and are susceptible to damage when taken to the pool or beach. Yes, water and sand are big enemies of these devices, since they can affect the laser and platter mechanisms. This winner cures those ills.

It includes a feature called ShockWave that all but eliminates the skipping associated with these portable marvels. It works by spinning the CD at an increased speed and constantly keeping ten seconds of music in its memory. When the unit is jarred, instead of experiencing silence in its headphones, you continue to hear music.

Other features include a water-resistant shell with special gaskets that seal around the CD lid and battery compartment to protect the unit from the elements.

It's colored bright yellow with black accents and operates for up to 10 hours on 2 AA batteries.

Best Mini Stereo System: JVC Executive Mini System

$350

Sized to fit in a bookcase or on a tabletop, JVC's Executive Series Mini System features classic styling that makes it a great secondary audio system for the home, dorm room, or bedroom, or a classic addition to any office.

Although small in size, this three-piece system is big on sound. Including the speakers it is a mere 6⅞x15¼x10 in. Nestled between the wood-grained speakers is a component rack that includes an AM/FM stereo tuner, a single-disc CD player, and an amplifier. Also included is an LCD panel that displays the operating functions, as well as a clock with alarm and snooze.

To increase the bass sound that can be missing from some mini systems is its hype bass circuitry, which boosts low frequencies without affecting the mid-range sound.

HOME THEATER PRODUCTS

As mentioned earlier, home theater is the hottest category in consumer electronics today. With the proliferation of video devices such as the digital versatile disc (DVD) and the small, unobtrusive satellite dish system as well as the bright future of the soon to come high definition television (HDTV), this category promises to get even hotter. That's because the video portion of a movie or television show is only one element of a good home theater. Good, well-balanced sound is the other. The addition of the right audio system gives depth to the image and creates an environment so exciting that you may never enter a movie theater again.

The manufacturers have finally realized that to bring home theater to the masses, it has to be simple to set up and operate. This has resulted in all-in-one audio/visual packages that allow even technophobes to set up in a matter of minutes. They have also introduced a number of these system packages that are affordably priced.

Confused? Don't be. Here's a primer for the first-time buyer, which explains the three types of home theater surround sound modes:

- **Dolby Pro Logic surround sound:** An affordable home theater surround sound. It takes stereo broadcasts and movies and converts the audio signal to an enveloping sound system.
- **Dolby Digital, formally known as AC-3:** This system is a digital step up from Pro Logic's analog and delivers digital audio to each of the five speakers—left, right, center, and two rear surrounds—as well as to the subwoofer. All Dolby Digital receivers include the Pro Logic circuitry as well. Dolby Digital requires an encoded signal that is found on DVDs and some laser discs.
- **Digital theater sound (DTS):** A newcomer in the sound field. Found in many movie theaters, this sound system uses less compression than Dolby Digital. One of the biggest supporters (as well as an investor) of this format is Steven Spielberg. Audiophiles are also supportive of this format.
- **THX:** Or as moviegoers know it, "The audience is listening." This format was developed by Lucas Films and, as rumor has it, developed after George Lucas walked into a theater to see the original *Star Wars*

and was appalled by the sound quality. The result was a system for theaters that would allow them to re-create sound to the moviemakers' preferences. When a piece of audio hardware features the THX insignia, it means it has met a minimum quality level. In simple terms, it is an enhanced form of Dolby Pro Logic.

Still confused? Don't be. Just stop by the local audio/video store and ask for a demonstration. Your ears will tell you the difference.

Best Value Home Theater Mini System: Aiwa NSX-AV800

$600

If you are looking for an inexpensive and space-saving way to get into home theater, then look no further than this system from Aiwa.

It features an AM/FM stereo tuner, a 3-disc CD changer, a dual-cassette deck, Dolby Pro Logic circuitry, a remote control, 5 speakers (2 front, 1 center, and 2 rear) and all the necessary wiring in one tidy box.

The receiver delivers 140 watts of power and it includes a three-mode digital signal processor for special audio effects. Best of all, it's sized a mere 12x10x13 in.

Best Step-Up Mini Home Theater System: JBL Simply Cinema Complete Home Entertainment System

$1,700

This futuristic-styled all-in-one system could rest as comfortably on display at the Museum of Modern Art as it would on your bookshelf.

Instead of a rectangular box like other mini systems, this model is wedge-shaped. It is 4⅝x10½x9¾ in. in the back and slopes to just 1 inch tall in the front.

It includes a single-disc CD player, Dolby Pro Logic decoding, an AM/FM stereo tuner, 5 speakers, and a subwoofer. It delivers 35 watts to each of the front and center speakers and 20 watts to the rear. Also included is a wafer-thin remote control.

Its small speakers can be hidden on any bookshelf while the rear speakers include mounting brackets for wall or ceiling installation.

What really separates this unit from others is that it also includes a 100-watt subwoofer that delivers Schwarzenegger-type effects directly to your living room.

HOME THEATER STEREO RECEIVERS

If you are a little more versed in audio you may want to build your own home theater system. The brains and brawn of any home theater system are the new audio/video receivers. A/V receivers not only provide AM/FM stereo and connections for your audio needs like CD and cassette players but are also outfitted with connections for your television, DVD player, VCR, and the five speakers plus subwoofer needed to set up an at-home audio/video theater system.

What also makes an A/V receiver different from your stereo receiver of yesteryear is it contains a decoder chip with Dolby Pro Logic, Dolby Digital, or DTS (or a combination of all three) inside, which allows for proper distribution of the surround sound for optimal movie enjoyment.

**Best Value
Home Theater
Receiver:
Sherwood/
Newcastle
Model No.
R-125**

$330

Sherwood has earned a reputation for building dependable and afford-able audio products. This entry-level Dolby Pro Logic receiver is no exception.

It features many of the same options found on units twice its price, such as gold-plated input/output jacks, a dedicated subwoofer output, rear and center channel controls, and a test pattern that emits an audible tone through the speakers to assist in setting up a well-balanced home theater.

It delivers 70 watts per channel in stereo mode and 60 watts per channel in Dolby Pro Logic surround mode. It includes an AM/FM stereo tuner with 30 station presets, a one-touch auto function mode that powers the entire system, and a remote control that includes a unique test-tone key for speaker balancing. It has 5 audio inputs, 2 video inputs, and 3 digital signal-processing modes (theater, stadium, and hall) for customized audio playback.

**Best Value
All-in-One
Dolby Digital
System: RCA
RP-9970**

$1,000

As mentioned, to take full advantage of DVD, you will need to pair it with a Dolby Digital receiver.

The best value package we've found is RCA's RP-9970. This is an all-inclusive assortment that contains absolutely everything you will need to upgrade your home theater to Dolby Digital—except the TV of course.

Included are a 200-watt receiver that includes an AM/FM stereo tuner, DVD optical and seven additional inputs and settings for Dolby Pro Logic surround sound as well as for Dolby Digital. Also included are five speakers: center, left, and right fronts, left and right rears, a powered subwoofer, and all the necessary wires.

But what makes this package truly extraordinary is its price—all this for $1,000. This is definitely the winner of the price is right award!

Best New Concept Home Theater System: Sony Power Cinema Model No. SLV-AV-100

$600

Sony's latest innovation, the Power Cinema, is taking the all-in-one home theater concept to the next level by combining a hi-fi stereo VCR with an AM/FM stereo Dolby Pro Logic receiver.

Measuring only 6¼x17x16 in., this unique combo-product fits easily in any stereo rack or A/V furniture ensemble. Because of its all-inclusive configuration this unit has numerous possibilities.

Not only is it an ideal system for the dorm room or apartment, it is just the ticket for those who want the maximum amount of features and functions in a little space—making it great for the bedroom home theater system as well.

Its four-head VCR features an eight-event/one-year programmable timer, VCR Plus+ for recording, and a remote with TV, VCR, receiver, satellite, and cable box controls.

Its stereo receiver has 75 watts per channel in stereo mode and 50 watts per channel for front and center, plus 25 watts for the two rear surround speakers in Dolby Pro Logic home theater mode. Other features include 7 acoustic custom sound modes (i.e., concert hall, stadium, sports) for more ambience when listening or watching special events, plus an 8-function input selector (VHS, TV, videos 1 and 2, CD, tuner, tape) for all your audio and video sources.

Even better, for an extra $300, Sony is offering a surround sound 5-speaker package, which includes 2 front, a center channel, and 2 rear— making this one of the hottest new concepts in home theater. Look for other consumer electronics companies to copy Sony and quickly jump on this VCR/receiver bandwagon in the coming months.

Best High-End Dolby Digital Receiver: Yamaha RX-V2092

$1,600

Yamaha's flagship home theater receiver is a technological marvel featuring state-of-the-art Dolby Digital audio output as well as other great movie watching enhancements.

Unlike other receivers, this unit has internal computer chips that allow you to listen to music or watch a movie in up to 13 different sound modes. Its theater mode includes a 70-mm movie sound field designed by Hollywood technicians that, when combined with the system's Dolby Pro Logic or Dolby Digital surround, multiplies the audio effect, bringing true theater ambience and sound to your home speakers. In addition, the unit offers a special sports program for stadium-like event sounds and 5 audio enhancements: concert hall, rock concert, stadium, jazz club, and church for customized ambience sound. The receiver delivers 100 watts to all 5 channels, has a subwoofer-out port, and second zone audio and video outputs for multiroom audio installations.

It comes with a sleek stainless steel learning remote with backlit display and 13 macro command functions. A companion remote for second room–system controls is also included. Other features include inputs for DVD/laser disc, TV/satellite, and two VCRs, an optical input option for DVDs and laser disc, and 5 S-video inputs. Audio inputs include tape, phono, tuner, and CD.

Best THX Dolby Digital Receiver: Denon AVR5600

$2,800

Destined to be on the wish list of every home theater aficiona-do, this powerful, THX-approved Dolby Digital receiver may keep you from ever wanting to go *out* to the movies again.

That's because it delivers a monstrous 700 watts (140 watts to each of its 5 speakers) and more A/V connectors than an AT&T switchboard. They include 4 digital inputs, RF AC-3 inputs for laser disc, 5 video and 5 audio inputs, 5 inputs and 4 outputs for composite video, and 5 inputs and 3 outputs for S-video. Other features include Dolby Pro Logic decoding and a remote control.

But enough of that unless you have an uncle named Trump and can afford a receiver with true snob appeal; this $2,800 system is the best of 1997.

SPEAKERS

Best Value Audio Speakers: Infinity RS 2000.6

$800

For a pair of great-sounding audio speakers that deliver lots of bang for the buck, check out the Infinity RS 2000.6.

Each speaker handles up to 175 watts of power and features a 1-inch tweeter flanked by two 6½-inch woofers for excellent stereo imaging and a solid bass punch. These speakers sound as good as others that are twice the price, and complement any center channel speaker, two rear surrounds, and a subwoofer if you wish to upgrade to a home theater. They measure 35x7½x14¾ in. and come with reversible speaker spikes for placement on carpeted or hardwood floors.

Best Value Home Theater Speakers: Cambridge Soundworks Ensemble IV

$400

Home theater speaker systems come in all shapes and sizes, but if space is at a premium, Cambridge's all-in-one Ensemble IV delivers big sound in a small package.

A great value as well, this assortment includes

five 3-inch cube-shaped speakers for the left, right, center, and two rear channels and a 6½x8x12 in. shoe box–sized subwoofer, all for only $400.

Although speaker cables are not included, wiring is easy. Just connect the speakers and the subwoofer to your audio/video receiver and you are ready to go.

Ultimate Home Theater Speaker Package: NHT-VT1.2

$2,300

For the more serious audio/videophiles, renowned speaker manufacturer NHT has assembled its VT1.2—a 5-speaker collection designed to reproduce state-of-the-art sound from both audio and video sources. Unlike some surround sound systems that are designed to be used mainly when watching movies and do not perform as well when you're listening to music, this package can be switched from video to audio playback mode for uncompromising sound from either source.

It includes two 38x5½ in. front tower speakers each with a unique, built-in side-loaded subwoofer that eliminates the need to add a sub to your system, a 5½x19 in. center channel speaker, and two 9x6 in. rear surrounds.

Best Outdoor Speakers: Bose 151 Environmental Speakers

$300

Designed to withstand even the harshest weather, these speakers feature a weatherproofed speaker driver and stainless steel grille that prevent rust and deterioration from high humidity and salt water—making them ideal for the deck, patio, or any outdoor environment.

Sized 6x9x6 in., each incorporates a 4½ in. driver and is rated up to 80 watts per channel.

Most Unique Outdoor Speakers: The Punkrock from Rockustics

$340

Constructed of a hybrid design material that looks like marble, the Punkrock looks great by the pool, hot tub, or in the garden.

Inside each "rock" is a weatherproofed 4 in. speaker that delivers up to 75 watts of stereo sound. They are designed for those who subscribe to the belief that "speakers should be heard and not seen," as they can be blended with the natural landscape. Best of all, they will surely be the topic of conversation at your next barbecue.

Also available is the Rockustics Plantone, a planter box with built-in weatherproof speakers.

PHOTOGRAPHY

Americans take over sixteen billion photos a year—almost four billion of them in the month of December alone.

However, unlike the consumer electronics and the computer industries, which dazzle consumers with new technologies each and every year, camera and film manufacturers have seemed content to rest on their laurels. That is until recently.

Last year a new photo format called the Advanced Photo System (APS) was introduced. The Advanced Photo System uses a smaller 24-mm size film format that is an evolution from the larger 35-mm standard. A consortium of manufacturers that include Kodak, Fuji, Minolta, Canon, and Nikon developed it.

Every Advanced Photo System camera features a slide adjustment that allows you to select from a choice of three sizes, from standard to panorama. This allows you to shoot different format pictures on the same roll of film. You'll also notice some major differences when you pick up the roll from your photo processor. Although you will still receive copies of each print, the negatives will be returned housed inside the film canister, along with a postcard-sized contact sheet showing thumbnail-sized images of each photo on the roll. The contact sheet is imprinted with the same code numbers as the negatives, so that you can match the contact sheet with the negatives with ease. In addition, each print will have a frame number and the date your photo was taken. To order reprints, simply give the film canister to your photo processor

along with the identification numbers of the pictures you want repro-
duced. That's the good news.

The bad news is that the photo industry did not adequately provide
or support most of the smaller local processors with the equipment necessary to process Advanced Photo System film. Since its introduction in
May 1996, only a few processors can develop the film, so trying to find
a one-hour or overnight photofinisher for this format is difficult if not
impossible.

But perhaps the biggest blow to the new format came out of left field.
Almost overnight, digital cameras became the hottest commodity in the
industry, and, struggling to keep up, the focus shifted (literally) to these
filmless wonders that almost instantly transfer pictures to your PC or TV
with no developing required.

When buying a digital camera the most important term with which
you'll need to be familiar is "resolution." Resolution is your best guide
toward determining the quality of the image and is quoted in numbers
such as "493 by 373," "640 by 480," or "832 by 608." These numbers
represent the number of pixels—tiny dots that, when merged together,
form the image. All you really need to know is that the higher the number, the more defined the image. All digital cameras come with software
for connecting the unit to your PC.

When you factor in the new photo-quality printers hitting the street,
I predict that the digital camera will be a major player in the photography field.

GENERAL TIPS FOR BETTER PHOTOGRAPHY

- First, standardize on a certain brand and type of film, whether
it's 35 mm or Advanced Photo System, and stick with it. You will
soon become familiar with its performance and limitations.
- Second, locate a good local photofinisher as opposed to using
mail-order or drugstore developing. To find a good photofinisher
call a local camera or photography club and ask for recommen-
dations. I always prefer a photo shop that has its printing and
developing equipment on-site, along with personnel willing to
take a moment to go over your prints and negatives with you in

order to give you tips on how you can improve your pictures. Yes, you will pay a few dollars more, but there is a noticeable difference in the quality of your images.

- Most important, don't be afraid to ask for help and suggestions. If the staff is "too busy," vote with your pocketbook and take your business elsewhere. Surprisingly, quite often "bad" pictures are not your fault. Most labs use highly automated equipment that is preset for the "average" picture and your prize photo of that great sunset may not look "average" to this automatic machine. Obviously, with the automatic equipment fooled, your print will not look as good as it should. A quality lab will be happy to look over your prints and negatives with you and, wherever their automated processors were at fault, make a corrected set of reprints at no charge.

35-MM CAMERAS

Best Entry-Level Point and Shoot 35-MM Camera: Fuji Smart Shot II

$60

For those who want a compact no-frills auto focus camera that takes good pictures and requires little effort to operate, Fuji's Smart Shot II is a great value.

At $60, this 4½ ounce pocket camera is the autopilot of entry-level cameras, with simple controls like a unique one-touch flash charge button on the front, automatic film advance, an easy-to-load 35-mm film well, plus a built-in lens cover.

Best Value Point and Shoot 35-MM Camera: Yashica T-4 Super

$130

At a street price of around $130, this is the point and shoot camera that I have recommended to many nontechnical friends. Almost everyone who has purchased the T-4 has told me "I never knew that I could take such good photographs." Many of these folks used to go on trips carrying huge cameras around their necks, some the size of telephones, when all they really needed was a good, pocket-sized automatic point and shoot model. Unless you are fairly serious about photography, you will probably get better photos with this type of camera anyway.

The T-4 is auto-everything and, most important, has a razor-sharp fixed focal length Carl Zeiss lens. Fixed focal length lenses are generally better optically in this price range, and their small size (as opposed to zoom lenses) allow cameras, such as the T-4, to easily fit in a shirt pocket or purse. It measures 2⁹⁄₁₆x4⅝x1⁹⁄₁₆ in. and weighs just 6.7 ounces.

One other tip for users of the T-4 and other point and shoot cameras: I highly recommend Fujicolor Super G Plus 400 film.

Best Point and Shoot 35-MM Camera: Contax T-2 Super

$1,000

The Contax T-2 is the aforementioned Yashica T-4's rich brother. The T-2 is the camera I would choose if I could have only one camera. It also easily fits in a shirt pocket and is the perfect vacation and travel camera. Like the Yashica, it is totally automated, but it does allow you a certain degree of manual control if you choose. The T-2 comes with a fast f/2.8 Carl Zeiss Sonnar lens with an ideal semi-wide 38-mm fixed focal length. Its body is clad in ultra-durable titanium, which makes it look so elegant that some say it makes a fashion statement in and of itself. Regardless of its beauty, it does just about everything right when it comes to photography. Many professionals carry the T-2 in a pocket as a second camera for that quick shot when there is no time to unpack and set up complicated gear. Believe me, this little gem gets pro-level results. Technically, it is classified as a point and shoot camera, but to me it is just too good to be lumped into that catchall category. If you can afford it, this is the ultimate highly portable camera.

Best 35-MM Camera: Canon EOS-1N

$1,750 (lens not included)

All right, the votes are in, not just from us, but from around the world . . . the Canon EOS-1N is the ultimate advanced amateur/professional-level 35-mm camera. How does this merit the highest ranking? Well, have you ever noticed all those huge, long white lens barrels pointing at the action during

sporting events? Those long white lenses are almost all Canons, and you see so many of them for one reason: they are moneymakers for professional photographers. The cameras and lenses used by professional photographers are their bread and butter. Pros will not jeopardize their incomes with inferior or unreliable products.

This camera features proven electronic reliability along with mechanical strength and durability. Its auto focus is the best in its class, and highly accurate as well. The camera can be used in either automatic or manual modes, and it includes virtually every desirable professional-level feature known. You can literally have it your way! The EOS-1N is next to the top (in price) in the large Canon family of EOS cameras. The EOS family ranges from the very inexpensive EOS Rebel series for amateurs to the more expensive professional levels. You can start with one of the less expensive EOS cameras and work your way up to a top model as your skills grow, with the confidence that almost all of the accessories and lenses you acquire will continue to fit your new EOS cameras as you upgrade. As mentioned, Canon has not only a family of cameras, but a family of lenses as well. Currently there are more than 50 lenses designed especially for the EOS family. Just like in cameras, Canon lenses range from amateur to professional (with prices to match). The finest Canon lenses are designated as the "L" series, and, if you can afford only one lens for our ultimate EOS-1N camera, I suggest the EF 28–70 mm-f/2.8L: USM zoom. It is one great lens and costs about $1,400.

ADVANCED PHOTO SYSTEM CAMERAS

Best Advanced Photo System Camera: Canon Elph

$500

Until the photo manufacturers resolve the processing dilemma with the Advanced Photo System cameras, it is difficult for us to recommend investing in this format. But if you don't mind waiting to get your film developed, then you will surely want to check out our favorite new Advanced Photo System camera: Canon's Elph.

This sleek, pocket-sized, point and shoot model is only 2½x3½x1 in. It features a pop-up flash and a nifty retro design and offers all the convenience (see above) of these new cameras. The Elph is housed in a stainless steel case and features a 2X zoom lens.

Best Use of Advanced Photo System Camera: Minolta Xtreem GX4

$150

This marine yellow underwater camera uses the Advanced Photo System film format and operates on land or under water, at depths down to 16½ feet.

Great for skin diving, windsurfing, boating, or just the family's beach vacation, the Xtreem weighs only 8½ ounces and best of all it floats, so if it falls out of the boat your photos don't wind up on the seafloor.

Other features include a built-in flash and auto focus.

DIGITAL CAMERAS

Best Value Digital Camera: Epson PhotoPC 500

$300

This pocket-sized camera looks just like a 35-mm camera, making the switch to digital less confusing. It measures only 3¼x5½x2 in. and weighs less than 1 pound. Its internal memory holds 30 images at 640x480 resolution. You can store up to 100 photos with a slide-in photo-span memory module for an additional $250.

The Epson PhotoPC 500 includes 4 AA batteries and features both automatic focus and a built-in flash. As an option, you can also purchase a unique snap-on LCD viewfinder ($200) that will enable you to preview images or view them once they have been stored in memory. Epson's PhotoPC 500 is bundled with editing and management software that is compatible with Macintosh and Windows operating systems.

Best Feature on a Digital Camera: Sony DSC-F1

$800

This model is the first on the market to feature a built-in IrDA-compliant infrared transmitter, making it capable of sending its images to a compatible notebook or desktop computer's photo printers without the hassle of cables or wires.

To transfer your images, just place the camera next to your computer or printer and press a button. The camera will transfer the photos in a matter of minutes. Allow me to note that although there are no wires to connect, it does take longer to transfer images via the infrared signal than it does with cables.

Other features include a swivel lens that allows it to shoot in a standard forward position and, by using its built-in 1⅘-inch color LCD, enables you to swivel it around and take a picture of yourself. Although I consider this swivel lens a frivolous feature that only adds to the price, it can be quite a conversation piece. Other than using the LCD as a viewfinder, it's also ideal for reviewing and selectively deleting the unwanted images you may have shot.

A lithium battery powers the DSC-F1 and it stores up to 108 photos at 640x480 resolution on its built-in 4 MB flash memory. The images can be downloaded individually or all at once. It is a mere 3x4x1⅜ in. and weighs just 10.6 ounces.

As a companion, Sony also introduced its DPP-M55 photo printer. This model can receive the images from the aforementioned camera without the use of wires or a computer but via infrared beams like your TV remote. Just say, "Beam me up, Scotty!"

Best Lens on a Digital Camera: Minolta Dimage V
$700

Digital cameras breathe new life into photography and this unit from Minolta is sure to be the hit of your next photo outing.

Featuring a detachable tethered lens, users can place the camera in one hand and the lens in another to shoot over crowds, around corners, and in confined areas. The lens can be up to three feet away from the body. Since the camera incorporates a 1.8-inch LCD monitor on its back, the user can see what the lens sees, even if the lens is placed out of sight.

Other features include a 2.7X zoom lens, a built-in flash, and a removable 2 MB flash memory card that holds up to 40 images at 640x480 resolution. It is compatible with Macintosh and Windows formats and includes all necessary cables for computer connection as well as the best photo software package on the market: Adobe Photo Deluxe.

Best Digital Camera under $1,000: Canon PowerShot 600

$800

If you're looking for higher-quality images, check out Canon's PowerShot 600. While other digital cameras take good pictures, this one, by today's standards, is an excellent choice for the high-end crowd.

Although the PowerShot delivers a whopping 832x608 resolution and holds 18 images in its built-in 1 MB internal memory, this camera also allows you to upgrade. For around $200, you can purchase the 4 MB memory card, which increases its capacity to 21 images, and you can even add a 170 MB miniature hard disk ($380), which allows you to store up to 900 images.

The PowerShot 600 also features a microphone enabling you to record a short narrative about each shot. The narrative can then be played back on a computer in conjunction with the designated photo.

This camera includes a docking station for easy computer connection, and the best macro function for its price—for clear, crisp, extra-tight shots. A nickel-cadmium battery and charger and Photo Impact Software are included.

COMMUNICATIONS

In 1876, the same year General George Armstrong Custer met his fate at Little Bighorn, Alexander Graham Bell patented a device called the telephone. Today Bell would be amazed. In his wildest dreams, I'm sure he never envisioned just how successful his invention would become and how it has spawned a revolution of devices like the answering machine, cellular phone, beeper, screen phone, and the latest generation of e-mail and computer phones.

TELEPHONES

Best Phone for Your Kitchen: GE Kitchen Phone

$60

The Kitchen Phone is the first telephone designed especially for use in the kitchen. It features an extra-long 15-foot tangle-free cord for easy maneuvering while preparing meals, a covered keypad that prevents your favorite spaghetti sauce or the kid's hot fudge sundae from damaging the phone, a built-in speakerphone, and a call waiting button on the handset. It is colored kitchen white.

Best Use of a Telephone: Telalert TA-2000 Home Security Phone

$250

These days, telephones can do just about anything. But if someone told you it could save your life, you'd probably laugh him or her out of the house. Well that's the case with the Telalert TA-2000, a combination telephone with a built-in motion-activated home security system.

Like a traditional phone, the TA-2000 connects to a standard telephone jack. It has an automatic dialer that allows you to input the phone numbers of nine individuals you would like to have contacted in case of an emergency. You then give these individuals a response code number. Incorporated on the front edge of the phone is an infrared motion detector. When it is set up and activated and when someone passes within four and a half feet of the phone, or when an emergency button is pressed, a 100-decibel alarm is triggered. At that point, the TA-2000 immediately begins dialing the preprogrammed emergency numbers sequentially until someone answers. It then plays a prerecorded message, in your own voice, alerting them to the intrusion. The recipient then enters the response code number and contacts the police. The purpose of the response code number is to ensure that a real person, not an answering machine, has received the message. A few years ago there were numerous emergency-type phones on the market that would automatically call the police, fire department, or hospital and play a recorded plea for help. Because there was no way for these departments to confirm there was an actual emergency, they were many times refused—making them useless in a real emergency. That's what sets this model apart. Because a live individual is making the call to the proper authorities, the call will be taken seriously.

Another feature of this emergency phone is its two-way open line feature. This triggers the speakerphone so the recipient of the call can listen to or talk to the base unit. It is designed to allow the recipient to audibly confirm the validity of an alarm message and assess the situation before calling the proper authorities. Included with the purchase are two key chain–sized devices for remote arming/disarming of the device. Additional accessory options include a personal medical alert button ($40), a wireless device that alerts those on the list of a medical emergency; a smoke detector ($60) that in the event of fire beams a signal to the phone, instructing it to begin the call initiation sequences; a remote infrared motion detector ($40) that can be placed in other rooms in the house; and door/window contacts ($40 each) that provide an alternative to the infrared devices and were designed for those who have pets that could inadvertently trigger the device.

Best Novelty Phone: Telemania Mickey Mouse Phone

$90

If you think phones are boring, check out this model from Telemania. Yes, it's Mickey, and not only does he look good, he's loaded with electronics that are sure to please.

When the phone rings, Mickey's head moves from side to side and his hand points to the phone while randomly reciting one of five preprogrammed phrases such as: "I think it's for you," "Oh boy, a phone call," "Oh gee, I wonder who it could be," "Well, what do ya know, it's for you," and "Hi-ya pal, you've got a phone call."

Other features include multiple ringer tones and last number redial.

Best Distance Cordless Phone: Sanyo Model No. CLT-966
$280

Cordless phones can be the ultimate convenience item or a certified pain in the neck. That's because more often than not these cord-free wonders tend to either run out of juice during an important conversation or make you sound like you're in a scene from *Smokey and the Bandit*.

Sanyo's cordless elimi-nates interference by using an

enhanced 900 MHz technology called digital spread spectrum to provide an operating range of clear, noise-free transmission up to a whopping 3,000 feet. Its extra-long seven-day standby rechargeable battery ensures that you won't get cut off unnecessarily.

Other features include a 20-number memory dialer and a unique speakerphone on both its base station and handset for hands-free operation. If you lose the phone, don't worry. That's because its base station has a find key that when pressed, causes the handset to beep until you locate it. Of course if you have a teenager you already know where to find the phone.

Best-Features Cordless Phone: Nortel Maestro 6300CLW

$250

Two years ago Nortel (Northern Telecom) introduced the first cordless phone that included a Caller ID display in its handset. This year, they are taking this technology to an all-time high by including circuitry that works with the phone company's new enhanced services.

Depending on the level of service you subscribe to, this 900 MHz cordless phone will allow you to not only see the name and the number of the person calling, but also to see the same information when a caller beeps-in on call waiting. While one button allows you to take the call waiting call, another transmits a prerecorded message to the party calling stating that you know the person is holding and you will be with them in a moment. If you have home voice mail, the caller can be routed directly to that service where they can leave a message.

It also comes with preprogrammed, one-touch network service access codes that allow users to activate services such as call forwarding and call return without having to remember the individual star (*) codes. Other features include a speakerphone, a numeric keypad on the base station, paging, and intercom capabilities.

For those not familiar with the phone company's new enhanced services, its Caller ID deluxe allows users to not only see the number of the person calling, but the name as well. Call waiting deluxe allows you to view the name and number of a person beeping-in when you are on the phone. For pricing, check with your local phone company.

CELLULAR PHONES

If you haven't jumped on the cellular bandwagon yet, now could be the time. There are great bargains to be had, and new features are making cellular phones more convenient than ever.

The cellular phone industry has matured to the point where its marketing strategy can be compared with that of the razor industry. Manufacturers figured out that if razors were sold below cost, they could make their money selling replacement razor blades.

In terms of the cellular phone, expensive phones are often sold for anywhere from $100 to $1 to free. Cellular phone providers then make their money on usage fees.

But it should be noted that the phones offered at these loss-leader prices are usually ones that have been on the market for a year or two. If you want a state-of-the-art phone, you will have to pay a higher price.

Also note that in some markets there is a new type of digital cellular service called PCS. This service adds numerous, previously unheard-of features to cellular phones such as faxing, e-mail, and pager functions, and most important, allows cellular providers to charge you for these enhanced services. However, at press time, PCS phones do not work in every market, and there are at least two competing PCS formats battling for dominance. If you travel with a cellular, definitely bypass this format for at least a year, as the PCS infrastructure is limited.

The bottom line is to shop around. The cellular business is competitive, so before signing a contract, let your fingers do the walking and compare the options.

When shopping for a cellular phone there are a few questions you will need to ask:

- How long is the battery life in both standby and talk modes?
- Are there different types of batteries available that will allow for longer talk times?
- How long does it take to achieve a full charge?
- How is the sound quality?
- Can the person you are calling hear you clearly?
- You'll also need to test the phone's ergonomics: Does it feel comfortable in your hand? Does it fit into a pocket or purse?

My favorite accessory for handheld cellular phones is an auxiliary microphone/earphone. This device plugs into the phone and allows you hands-free listening and talking but, unlike a speakerphone, the unit allows you to do so without others eavesdropping on your call. It's ideal for those who need to use the phone while driving. Auxiliary microphone/earphones sell for around $30 each and are available for most phones.

Best Cellular for Technophobes: Nokia 232

$100 (depending on service provider)

Any manufacturer that can take the fear factor out of new technology and make its product easy to use is a winner for me. That's the case with the Nokia cellular phone.

It features a large numeric keypad with the best LCD display screen on the market. It's small and lightweight too, measuring just 5⅘x2⅒x1 in. It weighs just 6½ ounces with the battery.

Other features include four programmable one-touch keys for one-button speed dial of your most frequently called numbers, plus a direct-dial key for 911.

It comes with a 40-minute talk time and 90-minute standby time nickel-cadmium battery.

Best Step-Up Cellular: Ericsson AF-738

$500 (depending on service provider)

Sized a mere 4x1⅞x¾ in. and weighing in at 4.8 ounces, this tiny model fits nicely in your shirt pocket, purse, or briefcase.

But don't let its small size fool you. The Ericsson AF-738 delivers 24 hours of standby and 90 minutes of talk time per charge. It features a flip-phone design that opens to reveal its mouthpiece and closes to protect the touch pad from being accidentally activated. Its speed-dial memory can program up to 99 of your most frequently called numbers, each up to 32 digits in length. It comes with a portable battery charger that delivers a full charge in 20 minutes and nickel-metal hydrate battery. However, when the battery has lost its zapping power, not to worry as replacements sell for $15. An optional desktop charger retails for $46.

Best "High Dollar" Cellular: Motorola StarTAC

$1,000

Dubbed the world's first wearable phone, this tiny (3⅞₀x1x1⅞₂₅ in.) flip-open model weighs a mere 3.1 ounces. The StarTAC fits easily into your pocket, or it can be worn on a belt like a pager. It includes a lithium battery that provides up to 1 hour of talk time and 12 hours in the standby

mode per charge. Motorola also offers an additional battery ($100) that works in tandem with the standardized battery to deliver a whopping 3 hours of talk time and 40 hours in the standby mode.

Other features include a two-line LCD, a quiet vibrating alert mode, and built-in security codes to prevent unauthorized usage.

Best Answering Machine: Casio PhoneMate TP-340 with Pager Link

$150

Keeping in touch while away from home is easier than ever thanks to Casio PhoneMate's TP-340 telephone/answering machine.

This sleek machine includes a new feature called pager link that automatically calls your beeper when it receives a new message. Although other answering machines have offered this function, they were complicated and undependable. Casio PhoneMate's entry, however, delivers the goods.

By simply pressing the pager learn button and dialing your pager, the telephone/answering machine automatically remembers all numbers entered (including the pauses), any personal identification numbers, and the alert number to display on the pager.

Fortunately, the Casio TP-340 also allows you to choose between being paged after every new message or only if the caller leaves an important message and enters the pound sign. The pager function can also be turned off completely. It works with any numeric and alphanumeric pager.

Its answering machine functions are digital—meaning it records its information on a tiny chip instead of tape. It holds up to 20 minutes of messages.

VOICE MAIL FOR THE HOME

The best answering machine on the market today is not a machine, it's a new service provided by phone companies called Memory Call. Although considered voice mail for the home, for me there is a difference between business voice-mail and home voice-mail.

Remember the good old days when you called an office and were greeted by an operator who could tell you whether or not the party you requested was in, and when he or she would return?

Technology has changed all that—and not necessarily for the better.

If you call an office that has replaced receptionists and telephone operators with a voice-mail system, you are automatically routed to an automated voice-messaging system. More often than not you become trapped, forced to listen to menu option after menu option. This wastes valuable time and, if you're calling long-distance, money.

Obviously, I am a huge fan of technology and what it has done to simplify our lives, but sometimes it can backfire and makes things more complicated. This is often the case with office voice-mail systems.

I used to feel the same way about voice mail for the home, but I'm starting to change my mind. Phone companies have been offering voice mail for the home for a few years now, but it has yet to become as popular as the old answering machine. I predict that this will change. A variety of new services are now making home voice-mail more efficient and effective than the standard answering machine. For example, some callers are turned off by call waiting—they think it's rude to be put on hold when another call comes in. Well, I'm no Miss Manners, but I think that it's okay to excuse yourself to take a brief message if your call waiting beeps while you're on the phone.

But unless it's an emergency, it's not okay to put your first caller on hold while having an extended conversation with the second caller. Now there is a new feature called Call Waiting Deluxe that makes the polite management of incoming phone calls a breeze. A digital display on these new phones shows you the name and phone number of the new caller while you're talking on the phone. This way you know who's calling before answering the call waiting beep. Even better, if you combine call waiting deluxe with the phone company's home voice-mail feature, the incoming call can be automatically routed to your voice mail if you decide not to answer it. Other advantages of home voice-mail include better voice quality, no machine to clutter your countertop, and no tape to jam or break. And, unlike an answering machine, your voice-mail system will continue to operate in the event of a power failure. Depending on where you live, home voice-mail may be available under such names as memory call, answer call, etc. But to take full advantage of this new generation of services, you'll need one of the new screen telephones. These new phones are called screen phones because the one feature all of the current entries have in common is a large LCD screen that allows each unit to accommodate a number of enhanced features. Most also feature a keyboard for typing.

Best Screen Phone: Nortel PowerTouch 350

$325

Marketed directly from local phone companies, this model is commonly private-labeled with the PacTel, Bell South, and

NYNEX nameplate (to name a few). Although it does not include a keyboard, it does include a large screen and uses soft keys that modify its functions to work with numerous phone companies' enhanced services.

For an additional fee (of course, be sure to ask how much these services cost), users can access stock quotes, sports scores, horoscopes, and national directory assistance listings right from their telephones. Although it can send and receive e-mail, it can be tedious to use, as the only way to enter alpha characters is with its numeric keypad.

Best Internet Screen Phone: Cidco iPhone
$500

This is the world's first telephone that grants full graphic access to the Internet. It incorporates a 7.4-inch grayscale LCD display screen and Internet browsing software that allows users to surf the Internet without the use of a computer. It has a built-in 14.4 kbps modem that the company touts as delivering the same page-to-page speed as a computer with a 28.8 kbps modem. This is attributed to the graphics being displayed in grayscale as opposed to color.

It features a smaller than usual but functional pull-out keyboard that allows you to enter addresses or e-mail text, and a cursor device that allows you to click on various links.

The iPhone allows for the use of any ISP (independent service provider) for Internet access. The providers are expected to enable Internet access via Sprint for a flat fee of $20 per month.

At press time when asked if this phone could be used to access online services such as America Online or CompuServe, company representatives responded, "There is no reason why the iPhone cannot work with these providers. However, there is no current agreement with specific Internet service providers other than Sprint."

Because it is a telephone, and not a computer, connection times are deemed to be quicker as there is no waiting for the system to boot-up. Initial set-up has also been simplified; all it requires is an electrical outlet and phone jack.

The iPhone includes an RS-232 port that supports a range of peripherals such as printers and smart card/credit card readers. These peripherals can be used to print out bank statements, Web pages, recipes, or other information found on the Internet.

On the telephone side, the iPhone offers enhanced features such as caller ID on call waiting, call forwarding, call blocking, 3-way calling, and call return.

Best Concept Screen Phone: 8X8 Via TV Executive Phone VC-200

$725

Giving new meaning to the term "screen phone," this futuristic "tele" not only allows you to talk to someone, but see him or her as well.

Instead of connecting to a television (see 8X8 Via TV, page 16), this high-tech–looking telephone incorporates a color camera and a 4-inch color LCD screen for true videoconferencing over standard phone lines.

Other features include a full-function speakerphone and a 500-number speed dialer. It is also compatible with the phone company's enhanced phone services such as caller ID and caller ID deluxe.

Best Computer Phone: Sybil

$500

Is it a telephone, or is it a computer? That was the first question I asked when I saw Sybil. What it is, is probably the most unusual albeit best new computer telephony peripheral I've ever seen.

Simply stated, this product is a two-line telephone that interfaces with a Windows 95–based computer. It features 12 interactive buttons that change depending on which button is pressed. Each plastic-encased button on the keypad incorporates a dot matrix LCD that is capable of displaying up to 14 characters of text or small graphic icons. They are even backlit, and change colors depending on which function is currently being accessed. Like its namesake, Sybil's personality changes depending on what the user would like it to do and which sequence of buttons is pressed. For example, in a basic configuration that is set up to be a phone book, the alphabet would be displayed. On the opening screen nine of the twelve buttons would be labeled A through I, another button would be labeled J through R and another S through Z, and the twelfth button would display "start again." The user simply presses the desired letter and the keys instantly transform into the names from your address book—one button for each name. If you have more than 12 names under a given letter, a "more" button will appear. When you choose a name, the buttons again morph into work, fax, car, and home numbers of the person. A press of the button automatically dials the call. Everything you need is conveniently packed into those 12 interactive keypad buttons we see every day of our lives. Sybil makes today's most complex computer transactions as simple as pressing a button.

The secret to Sybil is that there are no rules. That's because instead of being bundled with a dedicated software package, it includes a software developer's kit that allows any qualified Windows 95 programmer to make Sybil perform whatever complex computer applications a business or user may demand. This makes it an ideal product for companies servicing the needs of offices or value-added retailers who design applications for specific usage. The downside is that this is not a product a typical consumer would buy off the shelf and take home and use—unless he or she is a seasoned computer programmer.

PAGERS

When you stop and think about it, pocket pagers (or beepers) are amazing devices. With just a phone call, you can enter your phone number and have it magically appear on a pager's display—signaling its owner that you are trying to locate him or her. Depending on the level of service, that message could be transmitted down the street, across the country, or around the world.

Best Size Beeper: Philips Twocan

$200

This tiny beeper is no bigger than a car key. In fact it's designed to fit on your key chain.

It measures only 1¾ x 2¾ in. and is less than an inch thick. It features a single-line 16-character LCD screen that can store 20 messages each up to 240 characters in length. Other features include a backlit display for easy night viewing, user selected melody alert, silent messaging with vibrating alert, and both numeric and alpha message retrieval capabilities.

Best New Technology Pager: Motorola PageWriter

$400

At first glance the PageWriter looks different from other pagers. That's because it incorporates a unique tiny typewriter-like keyboard. This allows you to not only receive messages on its 2¼ x 1½ in. display, but send them to other PageWriters as well. This way, someone can send you a question and you can answer right back—without having to pick up the phone.

Its display shows up to 9 lines (27 characters per line) of text and is backlit for easy nighttime viewing. It also has the ability to transmit data via e-mail or to a fax machine. Sized just 3¾ x2¹⁷⁄₂₀x1¼ in., the PageWriter can be worn on a belt or placed in a purse. It is powered by a rechargeable NiMH battery that promises one week of service from a one-hour charge.

Allow me to note that because its keyboard is so small, it is a little cumbersome when typing long messages.

Best Practical Feature on a Pager: Motorola Tenor

$265

Like the aforementioned unit, the Tenor eliminates the need of a return call to find out why you are being beeped. However, instead of viewing a text message, this unit allows you to hear a voice-recorded message.

Here's how it works: If someone needs to contact you, he or she calls a phone number and simply leaves a message, like they would do on an answering machine or voice mail device. After the message is recorded, it is automatically transmitted to the unit. When it beeps, a press of a but-

ton allows you to hear the message. The Tenor holds up to four minutes of voice messages and selectively deletes messages. I have to add that almost twenty years ago I had a pager that received voice messages. But the sound quality was extremely poor and in many cases the message was inaudible. And if you did not hear the message when it was transmitted, you were out of luck since the unit had no memory. The Motorola Tenor caught my attention by delivering a very high-quality reproduction of the message.

SATELLITE SYSTEMS

Okay, the cable company has become the company you love to hate. But, in many markets that is changing. The images are becoming clearer, the assortment of channels better, and in some areas they offer cable modems that allow you to surf the Net at light speed. But, for state-of-the-art video and CD-quality audio, the new generation of small direct-to-home satellites are the best in the business.

First let me dispel a satellite myth.

Most folks (especially cable providers) say that if you get a satellite system you cannot get local television channels. But all three satellite providers offer network affiliates—odds are they aren't your local stations, though. This means that although you can get network programming, you will not be able to receive your local news.

The inclusion of the networks is intended for viewers that are not served by broadcast signals or do not have access to cable. The intent is to keep the satellite broadcasts from competing unfairly with the local stations.

But there is new technology in the works called spot beaming that could allow local programming to be delivered to your home via satellite in the future. I can only guess that this technology is at least two years away.

The good news is that every satellite receiver allows for an easy connection to cable or an antenna that, unless you live in a rural area, allows you to quickly and easily switch between the satellite and cable or antenna signal for local programming.

SATELLITE PRIMER

RCA DSS (Digital Satellite System): Consists of an 18-inch dish and a receiver that connects to your television. Its program providers are DirecTV and USSB. Initial cost is about $200 for equipment, about $150 for installation, and $350 a year for programming. Excellent CD-quality audio and digital video. 175 channels.

Primestar: Made its mark by renting—not selling—its elliptical 22-inch dish and receiver system. In other words, you do not have to buy the equipment, you just lease it. Primestar provides programming. It costs $360 a year for programming and $150 for installation. 150 channels.

Echostar DishNet: Upstart 18-inch dish provider. This David to the DSS Goliath sparked a price war last year that is still reverberating, making us consumers the ultimate winner. Programming is provided by Echostar. It costs about $200 for equipment and $300 a year for 175 channels.

Best DSS System: RCA 3rd Generation Model No. DS5450RB
$500

In its first year of production, Thomson Consumer Electronics (better known as RCA) sold more than 1 million digital satellite systems—making the DSS the most successful product launch in consumer electronics history. RCA's third-generation system is equally as impressive as its first.

This receiver has a new sort feature, which allows you to alphabetize the DSS's entire 175-channel on-screen guide for easy one-button scrolling and channel selection. A new surf feature brings up seven transparent channels at a time, allowing you to surf up and down the programming schedule while the current show you are watching stays on in the background. RCA has added its Home Director (see page 22)

feature to the DSS receiver and has also updated its parental control features, which now allow you to program specific viewing times for the little ones on weekdays and weekends. Best of all, RCA has combined a television antenna with its satellite dish, allowing easy reception of local channels without unsightly antennas or rabbit ears.

Best Alternative to DSS: Echostar DishNet

$500

Echostar's third-generation product incorporates some of the most unique consumer-friendly advancements on the market.

One of the features is a new on-screen program guide that not only lists the available satellite channels, but the local channels as well. This is a first for the satellite industry and is accomplished by having the user enter in his or her zip code during the setup procedure.

To access a local station, you simply use the remote control to select the desired channel. This instructs the receiver to automatically switch from the satellite input to the cable or antenna. Of course, the unit will have to be connected to an outside source (cable or antenna) for this to work properly.

However, Echostar is working on the process called spot beaming (described above) that allows local stations to broadcast its signal to its service area via satellite. This technology is causing the cable providers to cringe, as it could cut them out of the signal-providing loop.

Another feature, which promises to be a couch potato's delight, is its new caller ID function. Understanding that satellite receivers require the connection to a phone line for programming purposes, this feature utilizes this connection to display the name and the phone number of the person calling over the television image when the phone rings. Of course, you must subscribe to caller ID service from the phone company for this to operate properly.

Also included in this new model is a VCR recording event timer. This allows the user to place a VCR near the satellite receiver and, using the included remote infrared blasters, have the satellite receiver automatically set the VCR to record a desired program.

For those in search of the ultimate home satellite product, Echostar's Dish Network has introduced a new model that combines a satellite receiver with a JVC-branded D-VHS recorder. The *D* stands for—you guessed it—*Digital,* and it allows users to record a satellite program and play it back with near-perfect reproduction quality. Each tape allows for up to five hours of recording time at its sole speed setting. Although this unit can be used to play back conventional VHS tapes, the five-hour D-VHS tapes cannot be played back on standard VCRs. It sells for $750.

**Best TV
Antenna:
Terk TV 50**

$130

Forget those eyesore rooftop antennas that make your house look like a 1950s radio tower. The Terk TV 50 delivers the ultimate off-air VHF-UHF reception from a sleek 73x1 in. design that can be concealed flat against an outdoor wall, inside the attic, or against the roof eaves.

But don't let its small size fool you, this antenna is packed with state-of-the-art features like a two-stage amplifier that boosts reception and a built-in interference filter for clearer pictures.

Best of all, it comes optimized for DSS owners who have trouble picking up local stations. Its one wire solution DSS/TV installation kit features a 50-foot coaxial cable for easy one-wire connection to your satellite receiver or TV.

CHAPTER 2

Housewares

Remember the Mouli, the Vegi-matic, the Ginsu knife? What about the N'onion, the Juiceman, the Safety Can? Yes, no other industry can concoct more unique gadgets and inventions than the housewares industry.

Although some would claim that we peruse the aisles of the national housewares manufacturers, kitchen and bath, and the gourmet products trade shows for the free food (me) or the endless supply of coffee (Kelley), we are actually there to find the latest trend in kitchen products.

This chapter features a smorgasbord of items we've gathered and selected as the best appliances, cookware, personal care items, gadgets, products for entertaining, and much more for 1997.

So whether you're a seasoned chef or just the family's short-order cook, kick back and enjoy as we serve up our selections—prepared especially for you.

KITCHEN APPLIANCES

Whether it's a toaster, coffeemaker, microwave oven, food processor, or the latest generation of bread makers, there's always a kitchen appliance that will help you to prepare your favorite foodstuffs.

Best Value Toaster: Sunbeam Toast Logic

$30

Sunbeam has created its own window of opportunity in the toaster business with the introduction of its Toast Logic—the world's first and only toaster with a see-through window.

Located in the middle of this toaster is a rectangular window that allows you to actually view your toast as it browns—it's more entertaining than watching paint dry! But all joking aside, this unit makes great toast and includes advanced electronics that prevent power surges and other electrical interruptions from interfering with toaster operation and a computer chip that guarantees your toast will come out how you like it time after time.

Other features include an automatic stop button for quick release of the toast and a removable crumb tray for easy cleaning.

Best Toaster: Toastmaster Bagel Perfect Toaster

$69

After years of testing toasters that claim to toast bagels properly, I have encountered a problem: Although most new toasters feature wider slots that allow for the insertion of bagels, they toast both sides of the bagel simultaneously.

For a cut bagel to be properly toasted, it should be toasted on the face side and merely heated on the outside, not toasted on both sides. Although Bryant Gumbel literally "toasted" me on the air when I explained my theory, I am sticking to my guns and saying that this is indeed the proper way to toast a bagel. I have finally located a toaster that performs this task properly—Toastmaster's Bagel Perfect Toaster.

This unit has a nifty bagel switch that toasts two halves simultaneously. To use, just turn the switch to the bagel mode and place the bagel halves in the slot with the cut side facing the inside of the toaster.

The inside heating element toasts and the outside warms, the result being the perfectly toasted bagel. (This feature is also ideal for English muffins.) Even better, after each toasting cycle, the switch automatically returns to its standard bread mode so that you don't accidentally half-toast the next slice of bread.

Also available is a six-slice unit for $100.

Best Carafe-Style Coffeemaker: Black and Decker Kitchentools Model No. TCMKT800

$170

One of the best ways to keep your coffee fresh after a brew cycle is to brew it directly into a sealed thermal carafe. That's the idea behind this Black and Decker coffeemaker.

It features a sleek stainless steel carafe with a push-to-pour lid that seals in the flavor when not in use. Best of all, you can take your coffee anywhere, as the carafe keeps your java hot for up to five hours. Other features include a gold-tone filter, digital clock timer, and an automatic shut-off after each brewing cycle.

Best Speedy Coffeemaker: Mr. Coffee Speed Brew

$65

If speed is what you need to get a caffeine lift in the morning, look no further than Mr. Coffee's new Speed Brew.

Unlike other coffeemakers, which take seven to ten minutes to brew a fresh pot of coffee, this model produces a full ten-cup pot of coffee in about three minutes.

What makes the Speed Brew so fast is that instead of having to heat the water at the beginning of the cycle, it features a reservoir that maintains the temperature of the water at 190 degrees. This way, when you are ready to brew a pot of coffee and add the desired amount of cold water, the new water displaces the preheated water and pushes it over the coffee grounds. Hence, time is saved, as the water does not require heating.

There are a couple of drawbacks though: True coffee aficionados will tell you that coffee grinds need to rest in the steaming water for five to eight minutes and that the best coffee starts with cold water. Well, although this unit does not follow those rules, it is ideal for those who want coffee fast, or who, like John Kelley, make pot after pot after pot.

The Speed Brew also offers a vacation switch, which turns off the power to the reservoir if the machine will not be in use for several days.

Best Coffeemaker (Tie): Capresso CoffeeTeam and Cuisinart Automatic Grind and Brew

$230 (Capresso); $175 (Cuisinart)

For serious coffee drinkers who don't mind spending a little more for the freshest cup of java available, Capresso and Cuisinart offer the best coffeemakers on the market today.

The main reason that we selected these as the best of the year is that they both include our newest favorite feature: a built-in coffee bean grinder. This feature provides for the freshest homemade coffee available. You start with whole beans, have them ground upon demand, and immediately use the grinds to prepare the coffee. But instead of using a stand-alone grinder, and having to transfer the grinds from the grinder to the coffeemaker, these units do this chore for you. There are some differences between the two units, though. To operate the Cuisinart you start by filling its bean hopper with one tablespoon of beans for each cup desired—it can grind and then brew from four to ten cups of coffee. You then set the selector for the amount of cups you want and it's ready to go. After that, it does all the rest. It grinds the beans, passes them onto the filter, and starts the brewing process. To ensure the best flavor, its settings automatically regulate how much water passes directly onto or around the beans. This results in a full-bodied taste. Also included is a cleaning indicator that notifies you when it's time to decalcify the coffeemaker. All you do is put in a mixture of vinegar and water and the machine cleans the critical parts in a one-step method.

Although the Capresso unit is more expensive, it includes a bean storage hopper so you can pour the beans in, then set the coffeemaker for the desired amount of cups (up to 12) and strength. It then automatically takes the proper amount of beans and grinds them—this means no measuring. Its grinder is a Swiss Burr Mill and is the most durable on the market.

However, the Capresso unit does have more moving parts (meaning more could go wrong) because its filter mechanism automatically swings shut when the beans are ground inside and begins the brewing process. During our tests, however, it performed with flying colors. Both feature a strength selector, automatic shut-off, and large, easy-to-set LCD clocks.

Best Coffee/Espresso/Cappuccino Maker: Capresso C2000

$1,395

This Rolls-Royce of espresso machines not only makes the perfect latte and cappuccino, it's fully automatic, grinding the beans, tamping, and brewing your espresso all with the touch of a button.

Featuring an 18-bar power pump (a bar is a measurement in "cappuccino land" for power; 18 bars is the most power on a consumer unit), this machine allows you to make a single cup of espresso, two cups at a time, a 16-ounce cup of cappuccino or two mugs of coffee. It even has a hot water button. It's fully automatic—meaning all you have to do is insert the beans in its 10-ounce container.

Great for entertaining, its 96-ounce water reservoir can make 60 espressos or 19 cups of coffee continuously. Other features include a continuous steam release for cappuccino, a 96-ounce removable water container, a separate funnel for preground coffee, and an automatic hot water cleaning and descaling program that keeps your machine spick and span. Measuring 13¾ x 14 x 15 in., the C2000 fits easily underneath your kitchen cabinets.

Best Coffee Accessory Product: Larosta Coffee Bean Roaster

$150

If you're a beanhead, one who can recite phrases like "café mocha grande double latte" in your sleep (if you get any), then you'll love the Larosta, the world's first coffee bean roaster for your home.

By purchasing unroasted beans from the neighborhood coffee store or ordering them from a mail-order company, you can easily roast your own coffee at home. And because the richest coffee starts with the freshest beans, your coffee can get no fresher than this.

To use, just place 2.7 ounces of green coffee beans in the unit, adjust the dial for light, medium, or dark roasting, and turn it on—it does all the rest. It automatically separates the beans' outer husks in a stainless steel collector and air-cools the beans to seal in flavor. It takes five to seven minutes to roast a full pot (ten cups) worth of beans.

Best Coffee Grinder: Proctor-Silex Fresh Grind

$20

Because the freshest coffee at home comes from grinding the beans yourself, this Proctor-Silex grinder is the perfect coffee companion.

What separates this grinder from others is its unique internal cord wrap that winds the cord and stores it inside the unit. The grinder is also extremely versatile. In addition to grinding coffee, the Fresh Grind can also be used to grind nuts, herbs, or spices.

Other features include a stainless steel bowl and blades for easy cleaning, a safety control that operates the unit only when the lid is secured, and a large see-through lid so you can see your handiwork.

Best Hot Tea Maker: Cuisinart Perfect Tea Steeper

$60

If tea is your beverage of choice, Cuisinart's electric tea steeper makes up to eight 5-ounce cups of the best hot tea in about nine minutes using either loose leaves or bags.

Unlike other tea brewers on the market that use a dripping process, the Cuisinart model uses a steeping (or percolating) process to brew the freshest tea possible. It brings the water to a

boil and steeps the leaves by soaking them in the water for three to five minutes, depending on the desired strength. The user just presses the on button and the Tea Steeper does the rest. Not only is this unit easy to use, it delivers a brewed tea taste that is noticeably better than the old-fashioned tea bag method.

It also offers a keep warm feature that will maintain your tea at 185 degrees. The carafe has a dripless spout, an ergonomic handle, and can be removed from the heating base for tabletop serving.

BREAD MACHINES

Today's automatic bread machines give new meaning to loafing around the kitchen. That's because they have become the easiest method ever to bake a loaf of just about any type of bread.

These units first surfaced on the market ten years ago and have steadily risen in sales at the rate of 20 percent per year.

One reason for the bread maker's popularity is its ease of use. To bake a fresh loaf of bread, just pour the ingredients into its baking pan and press start. A few hours later, your bread is ready—it's that simple.

To make the process even easier, numerous companies have introduced prepackaged bread mixes—requiring only the addition of water and/or milk to complete the recipe. Premix packages can be found in grocery, gourmet, and department stores for two to three dollars.

What I like best about bread machines is the wonderful aroma you get when the bread is baking. Your kitchen smells like a French bakery, making you appear to your guests and family to have been working overtime preparing the perfect meal.

Best Value Bread Machine: West Bend Baker's Choice Plus Model No. 41090

$200

This unit looks more like a high-tech breadbox than a typical bread machine.

But what really separates it from the pack is how it prepares bread. While most bread machines produce a horizontal loaf, this model, with its rectangular breadbox design, prepares a more traditional vertical 1½- to 2-pound loaf of bread. Other features include a cast aluminum pan for crispier crusts, a large window and interior light for better viewing, a swing-open door for easy access, and two collapsible knead bars that minimize the holes that other units leave in the base of the bread. The unit has a dough cycle and seven settings for standard and whole wheat breads, including one for quick breads (such as banana or carrot) that do not require yeast.

Ultimate Bread Machine: Salton Breadman Millennium Model No. TR 3000

$250

Baking bread just went high-tech with this space-age bread maker from Salton.

This unit features a large LCD touch screen for its control functions instead of buttons and knobs, and is equipped with a computer chip which holds 12 to 20 built-in recipes. To operate you just press the screen, scroll through its memory for the type of bread you wish to prepare, and press the screen. In an instant, your recipe appears on-screen along with a complete nutritional analysis of the bread.

It bakes a 1-, 1½-, or 2-pound horizontal loaf of bread and also features a 15-hour delay bake timer so you can load your ingredients in the morning and have it automatically begin preparing your loaf while you work.

Best Microwave: Sharp R-330AK

$250

Microwaves are to housewares what cordless phones are to consumer electronics—the ultimate in convenience.

Sharp's latest microwave marvel features 1,000 watts of power and just about every bell and whistle available, including a unique LCD display screen that not only indicates the time and what's cooking, but also has an interactive custom help key that guides you through microwave functions with easy-to-follow cooking prompts. To operate, just press the help key and choose the item you wish to cook and the display may read: "Place on a paper towel," "Use large bowls," "Turn food over" and so on.

A built-in sensor automatically determines cooking or reheating times, and 12 one-touch instant start keys (i.e., popcorn, potato, soup) further simplify its cooking capabilities.

Other features include a childproof lock for safety and tamper prevention and a kitchen timer key for use with all your food preparations.

Best New Appliance Concept: Sanyo's Cord Free Collection
$230

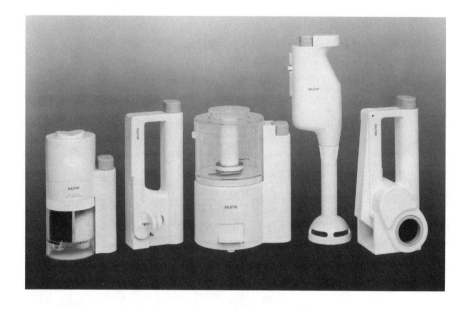

Another great idea comes from Sanyo with this cord-free assortment of five commonly used appliances that includes a can opener, a hand blender, a cheese grater, a salt/peppermill, and a food chopper/processor. What separates these appliances from the pack is that a single removable rechargeable battery powers all of the appliances.

That's right: one battery operates all five appliances (with more to come), making this the ultimate convenience package. Included is a battery charging station and a lightweight battery that quickly and easily slides into each appliance. Charging time is six hours, but since it includes two batteries, there is always a spare available in case the other depletes halfway through opening a can. Additional batteries sell for $20.

Best Can Opener: Safety Can

$20

This manual can opener does something no other can do: it eliminates sharp edges and the "disappearing top in your soup" syndrome.

Unlike other can openers that merely crack the top of your can, the Safety Can penetrates the outer seal of the can's lid, making a clean cut well below the top. The lid lifts off easily every time—sans sharp edges—and you'll never have to fish for it again.

Best Value Stand Mixer: Black and Decker Kitchentools Model No. SMKT800

$70

Any home chef knows what a hassle it is to stop the mixer mid-recipe just to add ingredients. This is not only inconvenient, but without continuous mixing it can turn your world-famous chocolate forest cake into a flop (literally). To the rescue comes the Black and Decker stand mixer that grants ample room to add your favorite ingredients while the beater still spins.

But that's not all. The bowl moves continuously, too, while locked into its rotating base, and the unit even includes a spatula attachment that fits inside the bowl and folds the batter back into the bowl, keeping it from sticking to the sides.

Powered by a 350-watt motor with 12 speeds, it comes with two stainless steel bowls (3 and 4.5 quart), a large beater, a wire whisk, and a dough hook for breads. Although the mixer is designed to fit nicely on your countertop, it has a hidden handle and cord storage if you prefer to tuck it away after use.

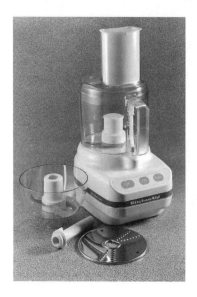

Best Food Processor: KitchenAid Little Ultra Power Model No. KFP350WH

$119

For serious chefs, KitchenAid's Little Ultra Power food processor takes the prize for its versatility and convenience.

Featuring a 5-cup bowl and a host of detachable blades and accessories, this food processor combines blending, chopping, whipping, slicing and mixing in one unit.

Unlike other single processors, KitchenAid has created a unique bowl-in-a-bowl system, making it literally two processors in one. Included is a 2-cup chopper/grinder blade and bowl attachment for smaller jobs and a larger 5-cup bowl with blade attachments. Now you can mince the garlic in the small chopper, remove the smaller bowl, and add your larger items for processing. Other features include easy to operate and clean front panel controls and a quick reference guide complete with recipes.

Best Turkey Cooker: Auto Chef

$150

Just as we were going to press with this book, a product that we have been anticipating for the past year suddenly became available.

Called the Auto Chef, this is the world's first self-basting roaster. Yes,

just in time for Turkey Day, this unique cooker consists of a roasting pan within a roasting pan that has a single mechanism that locks the two together. Running from the base of the pan to the top are two stainless steel tubes that extract the juices from the bottom of the pan every ten minutes and automatically bastes your bird or steer. Truly a technological marvel, it can cook a 23-pound turkey in 3½ hours as opposed to the normal 6. It saves energy too, because you don't have to open the oven door (allowing heat to escape) in order to baste your bird.

Best Oven: KitchenAid EasyConvect Oven

$1,550

One of the hottest (pun intended) new technologies to surface in the oven industry is a unit that combines both radiant and convection cooking. If you have an electric oven you may be familiar with standard radiant cooking that uses bright-red heated cooking elements. You may, however, not be as knowledgeable about convection cooking.

Convection ovens use fan-forced hot air to cook food. The two main benefits to convection cooking are faster cooking times (a five-hour turkey cooks in three hours) and lower energy costs. In addition, the end result is food that is juicier, crispier, and more evenly prepared.

The problem with most convection ovens is that they require different temperature and heat settings than standard radiant types. And trying to calculate these temperatures can require the skill of an MIT graduate.

That's what I like about KitchenAid's combination convection/radiant-heat EasyConvect oven—it includes a computer chip that does the math for you. All you do is select convection, punch in the recipe's listed time and temperature settings, and the oven automatically converts the specs from radiant to convection cooking times and temperatures.

Other features include a flat cooktop cooking surface, ergonomic dials with a large LCD window display, and a kitchen-white color scheme.

Best Dishwasher: Maytag IntelliSense
$800

This dishwasher incorporates a computer chip that acts as a dirt sensor that automatically determines wash times and cycle selections—really! It accomplishes this feat by detecting the density of food particles in the water and then automatically selects the necessary cycle for each load. When it senses the absence of dirt particles in the rinse water, it exits the washing cycle and moves on to the remaining stages.

Other features include a water-saving 6½-gallon capacity wash (as compared to the 9-gallon average), quiet operation, and an energy-efficient 40-minute (versus 63 minutes) average wash time.

Best Refrigerator: Frigidaire's Gallery Series
$1,500

Like other units that feature a chilled water and ice dispenser built into the door, Frigidaire goes one step further by including a built-in replaceable

cone-shaped water filter that reduces lead, chlorine, and bacteria levels before they reach your glass. Each filter lasts approximately six months (replacements sell for $15) and includes a date indicator to remind you when it's time to replace it.

Other unique features include built-in flip and slide shelving that allows you to adjust the shelves without removing them for easy storage of taller items such as turkeys, wine bottles, and two-liter soda bottles. Its large-capacity side freezer has plenty of room for all your leftovers.

Best Concept Washer/Dryer: Equator Clothes-Processor

$1,000

In the "why didn't they think of that sooner" category, Equator's new combination washer/dryer is the best idea in laundry since fabric softener. That's because it eliminates the need to transfer the clothes from the washer to the dryer—one piece of machinery does the job of two.

Designed for apartment-dwellers and smaller loads, it is 33x23½x23 in. In fact this compact unit with a front-mounted door fits under a countertop like a dishwasher.

In terms of savings, the Clothes-Processor only uses 13 gallons of water per cycle (versus 41 to 49 gallons per cycle for standard units), making it ideal for the energy-conscious consumer. And it uses 110-volt electricity, which means it can be plugged into any standard electrical outlet.

The installation has also been further simplified because it does not require a dryer vent. The hot air that is used to dry your clothes is cycled into a drum where it passes through a mist of cold water. This condenses the hot air which is then pumped from the machine through a water outlet. Lint particles in the dryer exhaust collect in the cooling water and are filtered through the drain screen as the water is pumped from the machine.

The washer automatically switches to the dryer by first preheating the laundry during the final wash spin. This warms the heater so that by the time the drying cycle starts, the heater is at the correct temperature. Drying then begins automatically.

The washing machine uses both hot and cold water connections and offers a choice of five wash and rinse options. The drying cycle can be set up to 120 minutes and includes two heat settings: 1,500 watts for nondelicates or 750 watts for delicates. As a result of the front-loader design, the horizontal axis (see page 257) uses a rocking motion to wash the clothes rather than an agitator—this prevents damage to your clothes. During the normal wash cycle, you have a choice between 1,000 and 500 rpm spin settings, which extract extra water from your laundry before it enters the drying cycle.

Best Kitchen Recipe/Shopping List Organizer: Brother Kitchen Computer

$200

If you're looking for the best way to collect, organize, access, and store your recipes, then your ship has come in with this electronic kitchen device from Brother.

Like a computer in your kitchen, this modern-looking countertop appliance takes up less space than a toaster and features a 7-line LCD black-and-white display screen and a reduced-size keyboard. It even has a built-in thermal printer.

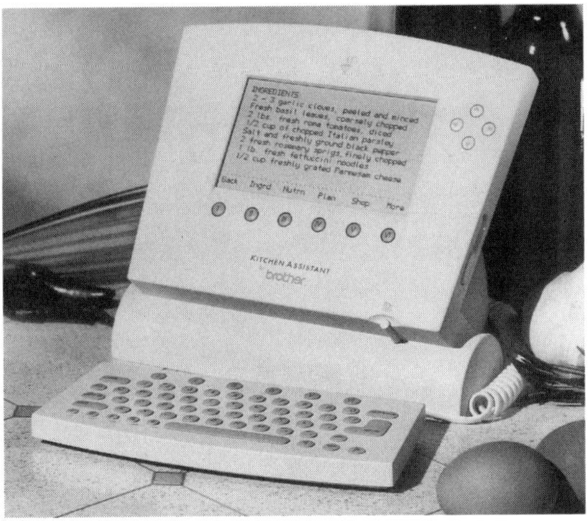

Included in its memory are 75 family-oriented recipes that can be displayed at the press of a button. It also allows you to plan meals for the day or week, create shopping lists, and even search your recipe collection by selecting recipes that contain only those ingredients you have on hand.

Other features include five independent cooking timers, nutritional analysis, and an automatic scaling feature that instantly adjusts the recipe for the desired number of portions.

Its printer utilizes adding-machine-size (2¼-in. wide) thermal paper that allows you to print shopping lists and recipes on demand. It runs on AA batteries or AC power (adapter included). Additional 32 KB (ROM) recipe cards with 120 preprogrammed recipes are $30, and 128 KB (RAM) memory cards that will be able to hold between 150 and 200 of your personal recipes sells for $40.

It measures $6\frac{1}{10}$x$8\frac{3}{5}$x$5\frac{9}{10}$ in. and weighs 2 pounds.

Best Way to Eliminate Plastic Wrap Cling: Franklin Wrapper

$30

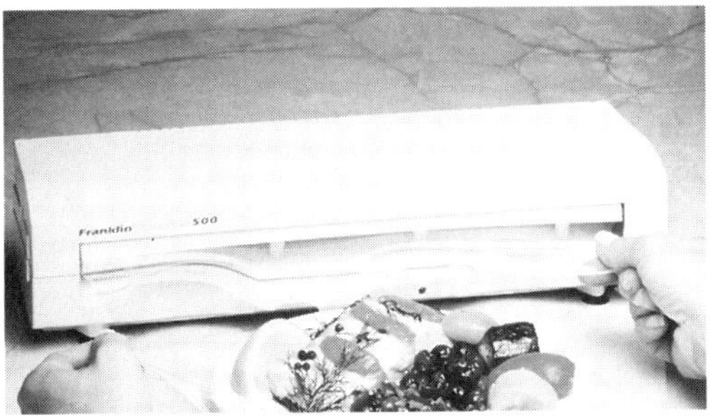

Does your plastic wrap cling together prior to usage—that is, when you are fortunate enough to be able to peel it off the roll in the first place?

Solving this dilemma is the Franklin Wrapper—an electric cling wrap dispenser.

To start, the ends of the wrap are secured by its lid, which makes pulling wrap off the roll a real no-brainer. But what makes this product really special is its cutting system. Instead of using a serrated blade, it features a small heated wire that is activated when you pull the wrap and cuts it like a hot knife through butter when pressure is applied.

It stores rolls up to 500 feet in length, operates on AC power, and includes four suction cups for a sturdy countertop mount.

PRODUCTS FOR CHORES YOU LOVE TO HATE

You know them, you don't love them, but somebody has got to do them. I'm talking about those tedious boring household chores we all love to hate. Whether it's ironing a load of shirts, vacuuming the entire house, cleaning the tub, or shampooing the carpet, nobody enjoys these household tasks.

But alas, some good news. We've assembled our picks for the best products to help make those dreaded chores a bit easier and downright fun. And if you believe that, then we have a bridge for sale too! But seriously, there are some great products available that will make your chores bearable anyway. Here are our picks:

Best Value Iron: Black and Decker ProFinish X750
$55

What makes this iron special is its distinctive sole plate that uses NASA's (that's right, the space program's) technology in its design to provide the smoothest way to iron fabrics.

When you combine

the sole plate with its 18-gram-per-minute steam output (yes, that's more than most), this unit delivers professional results at an affordable price. Other features include an automatic shutoff, a vertical steam setting for hanging garments, and an ergonomic rubber grip.

Ultimate Iron: Rowenta Steam Generator

$300

For those who take ironing seriously, this is the ultimate in luxury. This model is comprised of two pieces: a lightweight iron and a 33-ounce steam generator. The iron is tethered by a flexible hose to the steam generator and can deliver a whopping 1½ hours of continuous steam per refill. Even better, because it provides such a strong, constant flow of steam, this iron is ideal for steaming the wrinkles out of jackets, draperies, or just about any fabric. In fact, it delivers a better flow of steam than most dedicated clothes steamers. Simply stated, this king of all irons is definitely the best in the business.

Because the steam is generated in the water tank and transferred via its hose to the iron and not by dripping water on the iron's sole plate, the iron weighs in at a mere 2 pounds versus 3½ pounds for a typical iron. It also allows for steaming at much lower temperatures than most irons, which makes it ideal for use with delicate fabrics such as wool and corduroy.

When not in use, the iron cradles on top of the water reservoir for easy storage.

Best Value Vacuum: Royal Dirt Devil Ultra MVP

$180

Do you have to lug your upright vacuum up each step in your house when you vacuum, or place the unit on the couch just to clean the dust off your windowsills? How about cleaning those tight spots in your car's interior that seem virtually impossible to reach with the attachments found on most vacuums? Solving this dilemma is the Dirt Devil Ultra MVP upright vacuum with its unique hide-a-hose system.

With a built-in 20-foot telescoping hose, you can vacuum an entire flight of stairs without leaving the first floor. The Dirt Devil also comes with an edge wedge attachment and a triangular tool that store on the vacuum cleaner and connect to the hose for easy cleaning of corners and stairs.

Also included are dual headlamps, a 12-amp motor, and a stop brush roll position for bare floors.

Best "Lifetime" Vacuum: Kirby G5

$1,200

Many years from now, when some archaeologist uncovers our tools of the twentieth century, he or she, or it, will probably find a Kirby vacuum—and it will probably work too!

The Kirby Company has been in business selling its vacuums for the past eighty years. Their success lies in the fact that they only do one thing and they do it well. Unlike other vacuums, which have plastic molding or cheap hose construction, the Kirby is made of die cast aluminum, features a bulletproof hose, and has the best motor/suction power in the business (a true two-horsepower).

Although it weighs more than traditional uprights (23 pounds), the

Kirby has a foot-controlled gearbox for easy manual or self-propelled vacuuming in both forward and reverse. Other features include an accessory companion kit with more than ten tools and attachments for just about every cobweb and dust-removal job imaginable, a 32½-foot cord, a 7-foot hose, an upright bag, and a smaller collection bag that allows you to convert the Kirby into a hand vacuum.

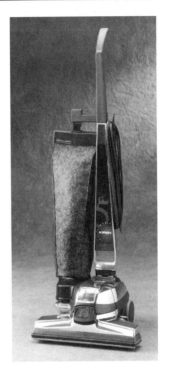

When you factor that the average consumer will purchase 10 to 12 vacuum cleaners over a lifetime, Kirby's $1,200 price tag doesn't bite too much either. But the best thing about a Kirby vacuum is its versatility.

A chameleon of sorts, the Kirby has a list of add-on accessories that convert its motor into more than ten different devices. They include a powerbrush accessory ($110) for hardwood floor waxing and polishing, a motorized upholstery brush ($59) and a dry-shampoo carpet system ($179). It even has a sander attachment! Its turbo accessory system ($94) transforms the Kirby hose into a powerful handheld sander with dust suction. There's also a massager attachment as well! What's next, a blender?

Guaranteed for life, and probably your kids' lives as well, Kirby vacuums are sold the old-fashioned way: door-to-door.

Best Multipurpose Cleaner: Bissell Little Green Plus

$110

Carpet cleaners can be valuable around-the-house tools. That's because when a spill occurs, these units provide a fast, easy method of preserving the carpet. However, my favorite carpet cleaners are not the big bulky units that take up needed storage space, they are the little ones that set up quickly and are easy to maneuver.

Bissell's Little Green Plus not only shampoos and cleans up small spots and spills on your carpet, it does windows too! Built into the unit is a 5½-foot flexible hose, 2 removable tanks (one for cleaning solution and hot water, one for the discharge), and a 20-foot power cord. Its onboard carpet/upholstery cleaning tool attachment consists of a 4-inch wide scrub brush that connects to the hose. You press its trigger to release a high-pressure spray that breaks down the stain and then draws the dirt into its discharge tank.

Its glass-cleaning attachment has a trigger and a squeegee with suction that allows you to spray a solution of glass cleaner and hot tap water on your window or mirror and suction it off. This eliminates the need for rags or paper towels and leaves a streak-free surface. Spring-cleaning was never so easy.

Best Bathroom Cleaning Device: Black and Decker Scum Buster

$60

Let's face it: When it comes to chores you love to hate, cleaning the bathroom has to be the most dreaded job of all. Tackling this headache head-on is the Black and Decker Scum Buster, a unique motorized scrubbing device that makes cleaning, well, almost fun.

Powered by Black and Decker's popular Versa Pack rechargeable battery system, this cordless handheld scrubber comes with three attachments: a 4-inch scouring pad for the tub and tile, a 2-inch-round detail brush for getting dirt nestled around fixtures and corners, and a short bristled 4-inch brush for cleaning the grout between your tile.

Encased in a plastic coating, the Scum Buster motor unit is waterproof and weighs only 1¼ pounds. It has an ergonomic handle for an easy grip and a trigger-mounted button (like a drill) for easy use. Each battery provides 25 minutes of run time (two batteries and the charger are included) and best of all, the batteries can be used with other Black and Decker Versa Pack tools and household products.

ENTERTAINING PRODUCTS

If I were Martha Stewart I would show you how to turn this book into a buffet serving tray, recycle it, and use it as a doily for your next barbecue. But I'm no Martha Stewart. Although I do like to entertain at home, unlike Martha, instead of spending tireless hours preparing the buffet, I would rather let the latest products for entertaining help me do the work—which is a nice segue to introduce to you the best products for entertaining of 1997.

Best Pizza Oven: Gino's East Deep Dish Pizza Kit

$100

If you've always wanted to be able to prepare true Chicago-style deep-dish pizza at home without the mess, this unit is for you! Licensed and tested by its namesake, the world-famous Chicago-based pizza restaurant chain, this stand-alone deep-dish pizza oven is the perfect product for preparing your favorite pies.

The kit includes an electric 12-inch-round, 1½-inch-deep nonstick aluminum cooking surface with an embedded heating element and a lid. All you do is prepare the dough, add the ingredients, and close the lid. Because of its tight-sealing lid, a loaded deep-dish pizza is ready in 20 minutes.

But best of all, Gino's is supplying pizza ingredients (five pack: $25) including special prepackaged flour mixes from its restaurant for authentic New York, Chicago, and whole wheat–style pizzas, plus recipes that provide super pies for the Super Bowl.

Best Food Warmer: Metrokane Hot Butler

$50

This is definitely the coolest "hot" product I've seen in a long time! Instead of using Sterno, alcohol, or electricity to keep food warm, this unique buffet warmer uses two tiny tea candles (included).

It features a black 16x12 in. super-conductive aluminum top that absorbs the heat from the candles below and keeps the tray at an even 175 degrees for up to five hours.

Just place the unit on your table and light the two candles. About five minutes later, lower the hinged tray so it can begin absorbing the heat, and place your hors d'oeuvres, casserole, or serving dish on top.

The Hot Butler's base stays cool on any surface, including wood and tablecloths.

Best Big Buffet Server: West Bend Buffet Server

$210

For larger gatherings, you may want to take a look at West Bend's Buffet Server. This 22x10 in. stainless steel tray holds one 3-quart and two 1½-quart dishes. Each dish is removable for easy cleaning and features lids that help keep the food warm.

An adjustable temperature control allows you to set the temperature between 165 and 185 degrees. It runs on AC power and easily converts into a warming tray.

Best Indoor Grill: T-Fal Compact Grill

$75

Everyone loves a good barbecue. But, if the weather is not cooperating or you just don't feel like fighting the bugs for your meal, then an indoor grill may be just the ticket.

Today's batch of indoor grills are smokeless—making them ideal for year-round fun. Our pick for this year's best is T-Fal's Compact Grill. This AC-powered unit features an 81-square-inch nonstick cooking grate that is grooved and angled to channel fat and grease away from the food. Since the fat and grease never touch the heating elements, it prevents smoke from forming indoors. Because of its 10x16x3 in. size, it can be placed on the kitchen counter or directly on the dining room table.

Best New Wine Product: Vintage Enhancer

$60

This late entry in the book is the most unusual gadget we've seen in a long time.

Called the Vintage Enhancer, it actually ages wines, liquors, and brandies. Yes, now you can take the cheap stuff and make it the good stuff in less than 30 minutes.

It consists of an electric chrome-plated device that looks like a fancy wine cooler. To use, just place a bottle of wine, liquor, or brandy in the enhancer. It then emits a low amp magnetic wave that changes the ionic charge of acids and tannins that affect the flavor of your favorite alcoholic beverages. It makes them taste as if they have been aged for years without affecting the alcohol content.

For red wines, the Vintage Enhancer breaks down the tannic acid much like aging does over time. The enhancer doesn't age the wine, but it takes a highly tannic wine and makes it taste like it's five years older in just 30 minutes. Of course different wines have different tannic levels. So if you open a bottle and don't like the taste, put it in the enhancer.

Alcoholic beverages such as scotch, whiskey, bourbon, and cognac have acids as well. The enhancer can take a five-year-old bottle of scotch, alter the acids, completely mellow its strong bite, and make it taste like a twenty-year-old bottle.

And during a recent *Today* show segment we put a bottle of grapefruit juice in the Enhancer, and after twenty minutes we found that the juice was smoother and less acidic.

Pie in the sky? Who knows? But we do have it on good authority that the scientific process used is valid.

OUTDOOR ENTERTAINING

Whether it's a tailgate party in the parking lot, a backyard barbecue, or a picnic in the park, the latest products for the great outdoors are guaranteed to please.

Best Gas Barbecue Grill: CharBroil Saber

$679

The one factor most barbecue grills have in common is that they are a pain to keep clean. That's where this new model from CharBroil excels. Although it is made of stainless steel, both the exterior and the cooking grate are coated in porcelain, making them a snap to wipe clean. The porcelain coating also makes it virtually impervious to rust—meaning that it could outlive us all. But that's the trick behind barbecuing—long life. The best-tasting barbecue fare comes from older grills that have been seasoned with use. So when shopping, make sure that the grill is durable enough to last numerous seasons—this one passes that test easily.

Underneath the grill are shelves, a paper towel holder, and a swing-out condiment rack. Also included is a rotisserie attachment that connects to the burner for easy vertical grilling of chicken and other meats. It has a 543-square-inch cooktop, a side burner, and a cutting board as well.

Best Portable Barbecue Grill: Keg A Cue

$50

If John Madden needed a portable barbecue grill, this is the one he would want! Although this item looks like a beer keg, it opens to reveal a portable charcoal grill. Great for the beach, a picnic, or a parking lot, this three-piece 17-pound grill features a steel top with a built-in handle for easy carrying. It has a 13x15 in. grilling surface that provides enough room for a dozen burgers, and it has a steel base with two retractable legs. Needless to say, it is also a conversation piece.

Best Portable Cooking Product: Max Burton Max Pack

$150

This is my definition of roughing it—an all-in-one system that makes life at the campground, picnic, or tailgating event a true first-class experience. The Max Pack includes a tabletop burner, a stovetop grill, and a unique collapsible lantern—all packed in one easy-to-haul nylon bag.

The square gas grill features three heat settings and, like the lantern, is powered by butane (which comes in easy-to-transport canisters). The stovetop grill add-on rests above the gas burner and includes a disk-shaped angled cooking surface that allows unwanted fat to drain away from the food and into a holding area for easy cleanup.

Best Blender for Your Car: Waring Tailgater

$140

Tailgaters never cease to amaze me. If you haven't been to a tailgating party lately, boy have you missed out. These folks not only know how to party, they know how to eat! They assemble before a sporting event and convert their cars and trucks into mobile gourmet buffets. This year's best blender for a tailgating event is Waring's (aptly named) Tailgater.

Designed for those who want to blend their own frozen concoctions while waiting for the game to start, this 45-ounce capacity two-speed blender is shatterproof and comes with an extra-long 15-foot cord that plugs into your car's cigarette lighter so you can mix and mingle at the same time.

Best Beverage Cooler: Rubbermaid Anything Goes

$60

If you've ever struggled with hauling a loaded ice chest from one point to another, you know just how heavy these things can get. Although the Rubbermaid Anything Goes was introduced three years ago, it is still the best large cooler on the market.

What separates this one from the pack is that it includes wheels and a retractable handle that makes pulling around a load of iced canned drinks a snap. Why is it so easy to lug around? The wheels. You may or may not know that Rubbermaid also owns

Little Tykes. This company is famous for high-quality plastic toys and playhouses. Little Tykes's number one selling item is the Cozy Coupe—a small foot-powered indoor/outdoor car for kids. A couple of years ago, to demonstrate just how many Cozy Coupes have been sold, Rubbermaid announced that it was the number one selling car in the USA. They have outsold both the Ford Taurus and the Honda Accord.

Okay, enough of the trivia—now back to the Anything Goes.

It has a giant 60-quart capacity and includes two cooling packs that snap into its lid. Simply stated, it has enough capacity to hold an entire picnic buffet, and even allows those gigantic two-liter soft drink bottles to stand in an upright position.

PERSONAL CARE

Take a look around your bathroom. Is your hair dryer beginning to sputter? Is your razor cutting more skin than hair? Or does your toothbrush look more like a thistle than a dental care product?

If so, don't worry, the personal care arena has entered the space-age with new offerings that not only simplify usage but also make your current items seem antiquated in comparison. Here are our picks for the best.

Best Blow Dryer: Conair Anti-Static Dryer

$30

Although my receding hairline attests to the fact that I personally do not need to rely on a hair dryer, the folks at Conair have developed a new model that even I can appreciate.

That's because it not only dries your hair (or, in my case, hairs), it is the first dryer that removes static in the process. Called (appropriately) the Anti-Static Dryer, this powerful 1,600-watt model features a built-in crystal that emits negative ions while drying (really!). The crystal eliminates static electricity (positive ions) that builds up and causes static in your hair. To activate, just squeeze the handle located on the grip of the dryer.

Please note that I did not personally test this unit, and because Kelley doesn't blow-dry his hair, we delegated this task to Julia Furr, a staffer who does, in fact, have hair.

She reports that this product not only prevented the static buildup, it was so powerful it dried her abundance of hair much more quickly than other hair dryers. Other features include two heat settings and a cool-shot button for styling.

Best Bathroom Scale: T-Fal Evidence IMC

$120

If you're like me and find it increasingly difficult to see those tiny numerals on the bathroom scale, don't worry, help is on the way.

While standard bathroom scales force you to look down to try to read the ever-shrinking display dial, the Evidence IMC (intuitive memory concept) solves this problem by separating the weighing mechanism and numerical display into two parts. The weighing mechanism goes on the floor and its LCD screen mounts on the wall at eye level. This wall module receives infrared signals from the weighing mechanism and displays your weight on its screen—making it easier for those of us with aging eyes to see the true figures. Even better, the scale remembers up to four different users' weights, and can display how much has been lost or gained since the last weigh-in—that is, if you want to be reminded of that pizza you had for lunch.

Best Electric Razor: Norelco Tripleheader Model No. 5885XL

$150

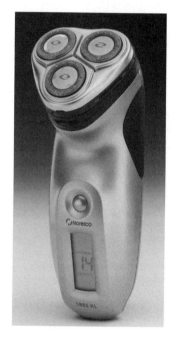

For the closest shave ever (okay it's cliché but how original can you get with an electric razor), check out the Norelco Tripleheader. This cordless razor is truly up to Pargh. I've been using it for about six months and it definitely delivers the best electric shave on the market.

And yes, electric razors provide just as close a shave as a blade. However, your face has to adjust to electric razors. That means it takes about two weeks to condition your beard to an electric unit. After that, you can throw out all your creams and razors and plug in to the most convenient method of shaving.

Besides its excellent shave, what I like about the Norelco is its ergonomic large rubber grip that fits in the palm of your hand and its LCD display that indicates via an audible tone how many shaves are left, the remaining power in batteries, and when to clean the razor.

The razor has 45 lifters and 45 rotating blades that lift first, then cut your stubble for a close shave without irritation, and a pop-out trimmer for mustaches, beards, and sideburns.

It comes with a worldwide voltage cord, which adjusts automatically from 100 to 240V AC/DC and includes a travel carry case, shaving head cap, and coil cord.

Best Shower Massager Device: Hansgrohe Aktiva Caresse

$130

If you've ever owned a massaging shower head, then you've no doubt noticed that over time, your invigorating massage gets less and less powerful, eventually leaving you with a mere trickle of its former self. That's because mineral deposits and chemicals in your water clog the heads.

To the rescue comes the Hansgrohe Aktiva Caresse, the world's first self-cleaning hand shower. Water-driven gears that spin inside the showerhead power its innovative turbo-clean feature. As the gear heads rotate, cleaning pins are pushed through alternating sections of the spray channels. The result is that the showerhead stays clean, ensuring maximum water output while the turbines create an invigorating massage. Best of all, you'll never have to stick a toothpick in those tiny holes again!

Best Electric Toothbrush: Braun Oral-B Ultra Plaque Remover

$90

Although the Oral-B electric toothbrush was introduced in 1991, Braun has managed to maintain its dominance over many imitators by consistently improving an electric toothbrush's most important feature: speed.

Braun's latest generation of its Oral-B electric toothbrushes, the Ultra, is no exception.

Its superfast oscillation helps remove heavy plaque buildup and stains. It also has a unique cupped brush head that surrounds each tooth in a similar fashion to a dental instrument, providing you with a professional clean. Another unique feature is its built-in timer that signals you by staggering the brush head's speed when you have reached the dentist's preferred brushing time of three minutes.

There is bad news, though: The brush heads wear out pretty fast, and replacements are expensive—about $14 each.

Best Toilet Paper: NuWay Moist Mates

$2 (original); **$3** (medicated); **$1.40** (refills)

When we say that we travel to all *ends* of the earth to find the latest and greatest products, we mean it literally. Case in point, we present the world's only moist toilet paper on a roll from NuWay.

You may think we have hit rock bottom with this one, but these innovative rolls of paper just could be the Post-it notes of the bathroom. Each roll of Moist Mates comes in a refillable protective plastic dispenser that piggybacks below your existing toilet paper roll. Available in two varieties, original and medicated, they consist of a roll of 80 standard-size sheets. They are hypoallergenic, environmentally safe, flushable, and biodegradable.

BABY PRODUCTS

Are you having a baby, or do you know someone who is? If so, choosing the right product for the little one is a difficult if not impossible task.

The hard part is wading through the vast assortment of available items to find the perfect product.

To aid your shopping chores, check out some of our picks for the best.

Best Concept Baby Product: BumpaBed

$219 (mattress, two sheets, board, insert

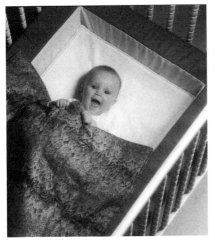 

If you are searching for the latest in baby bedding, look no further than the BumpaBed. This is a unique combination crib mattress and bumper guard that not only makes the tyke comfortable, but also protects him or her from accidentally falling overboard. It consists of soft, fire-resistant foam that, unlike traditional baby mattresses, has been hollowed out to provide a cozy, padded sleeping nook. Its hollowed-out design also creates a smart bumper system. But what really makes this something that only a parent could love is its removable bottom sheet system. Instead of having to constantly change and retuck the bottom sheet, it is attached with hook and loop fasteners. This way, when it's time to change the bed, just zip off the old sheet and press on the new one. It fits inside most standard-size cribs and is portable enough to be the ideal bed for an overnight stay at Grandma's. As the child grows, you can place a filler mattress inside the hollowed-out area and quickly and easily create a toddler bed. There is also an optional wooden couch accessory available ($190) that converts the unit into a 4-foot-long futon-style couch/bed. But probably the one use that only I could think of for this product is that it also makes the ideal indoor pet bed. In fact, my huge German shepherd, Einstein the Wonderdog, sleeps in one every night. Trust me, if he did not like it, it would be in pieces by now!

Best Baby Sleep Product: Norelco Nap Time Sounds

$65

To help your baby fall asleep comes this 5x7 in. plastic picture frame that not only holds a photo of Mom and Dad, but also incorporates a sound conditioner that emits soothing sounds that mask unwanted or distracting noises. It allows you to select from five patterns ranging from rain and ocean wave to a lullaby and a heartbeat that are designed to relax the baby and lull him or her to sleep.

The frame is decorated in comforting pink and blue cosmic motif and includes a 60-minute timer, volume control, and a night-light.

Best Baby Bath Product: Peek's Bath Monitor

$15

As new parents will quickly learn, setting the bathwater at just the right temperature can be difficult. That's where the Peek's new Bath Monitor comes into play. This is a hockey puck–sized float-

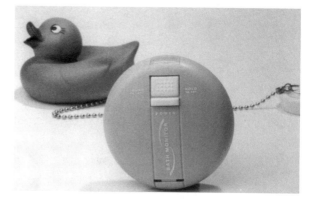

ing temperature device that tells you when the water is at the perfect temperature. Here's how it works: To initially set the unit, you need to draw a bath to the proper temperature. Then you place the Bath Monitor in the water and press its set button until its green light illuminates. This allows the unit to memorize the proper temperature.

The next time you run a bath just place the Bath Monitor into the water. If the water is too warm, it will beep and illuminate a red light. If it is too cold, a yellow light will come on. The manufacturer claims that it is accurate to +2 or -4 degrees. Its temperature range is 40 to 120 degrees.

The Bath Monitor operates on one 9-volt battery, which will last up to 150 baths.

Best Stroller: Cosco Rock N Roller

$120

This stroller not only strolls, it rocks, glides, and transforms into a bassinet.

Designed for newborns and toddlers up to 40 pounds, this 6-wheeled stroller (4 front and 2 rear) can be used as a rear-facing carriage (bassinet) for infants or, with the touch of a button, can be flipped around to create a front-facing seat for toddlers. Even better, its bassinet lifts out so you can bring baby inside and rock him/her to sleep.

Other features include a rocking chair–like motion for toddlers in the front facing position that, when flipped toward the rear, converts into a glider for babies. Of course it locks into a stationary position as well. Also included is a fold-up roof and plenty of storage space for toys, bottles, and diapers underneath.

Best Safety Bath Product: First Alert Expandable Bath Seat

$18

Because wet babies are difficult, if not impossible, to bathe and hold at the same time, First Alert developed this unique chair for the baby's bath.

It features three suction cups on its underside to keep the chair in place and a high chair–style tray that prohibits the child from squirming out of the unit. The tray adjusts to facilitate entry and removal, and to accommodate a growing child.

The First Alert Expandable Bath Seat weighs 1.9 pounds and is intended for children who are old enough to sit up on their own.

Best Idea Baby Product: Umix Shake It Up Baby Bottle

$6

Any parent that has tried to mix water and formula in one hand while juggling junior in the other will love this revolutionary new baby bottle from Umix.

What makes the Shake It Up unique is that it has dual chambers that allow you to store powdered formula in one chamber and water in another. When that predawn feeding time hits, just unlock the chamber, shake, and serve. This is especially helpful for baby-sitters, caregivers, or traveling parents as it eliminates the need for refrigeration until after the bottle is mixed.

Best Baby Monitor: First Alert Clear Sound Nursery Monitor

$80

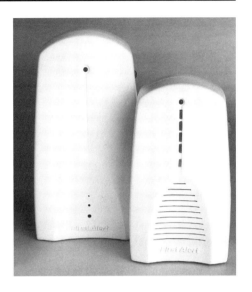

This year's best nursery monitor is First Alert's Clear Sound Nursery.

What separates this two-piece audio monitor from the pack is its unique receiver device. Instead of a big bulky device, this unit looks like a beeper and even comes with a built-in clip so you can wear it on your belt. Other features include an out-of-range and battery-low indicator light plus a unique sound intensity LED display with four red indicator lights that give you a visual indication of how loud a sound your child is making. This is especially helpful if you're in a loud room or not within earshot of the receiver.

PET PRODUCTS

Best Cat Litter Box Product: Litter Maid

$200

Designed for the cat who has everything, this space-age electric litter box brings new meaning to the word "automation."

That's because it cleans itself—really! All you have to do is add clumping-style litter and occasionally empty a sealed container.

The litter box features an electronic sensor that detects when the cat has done its business. Ten minutes after your pet has left the facility, a combing device moves from one end to the other and pushes the waste (which has clumped together) into an airtight disposable container. The Litter Maid operates on an AC adapter (included) or 8 D-cell batteries (not included). It is 24x17x9 in.

Best Cat Water Bowl: Drinkwell Pet Fountain

$40

Created by a veterinarian, the Drinkwell is designed to prevent kitty's water from becoming stagnant and crystallized, thereby reducing your cat's chances of getting a urinary tract infection.

To use, just fill the container with five cups of water and turn the unit on. The motor continuously circulates the water from the filter to the dish and back again.

The unit is 10x7x7 and includes a dish. The motor's 6-foot cord plugs into a standard electrical outlet and is designed to run continuously. Filters last for 6 to 8 weeks and replacements sell for $4.

Best Pet Collar: Saving Pet Light

$8

The best way to show your affection for your pets is with a gift that helps keep them safe.

The Saving Pet Light is a 1½-inch flashing red light that attaches to your pet's collar. When exposed to dimly lit situations, it automatically

begins an illuminating flashing cycle that continues until the animal enters a lit area or lies down for a period of more than 15 seconds.

The light is designed to make your pet more visible to oncoming traffic or passersby, and it can be seen up to a third of a mile away. Two button-cell batteries (included) power the unit for up to 100 hours.

The Saving Pet Light is water-resistant and fits any collar.

Best Dog Bowl: Virtu Flexo Feeder

$30

Because all dogs are not the same size, this flexible dog bowl holder allows you to provide the best feeding height for your dog to more easily digest its food.

Made of a flexible plastic material, it holds one pet bowl and can be elevated from 10 to 22 inches, and it comes with a plastic water bottle for travel as well.

Best Pet Brush: Wahl Electric Detangling Comb

$100

Most pets enjoy a good brushing—that is, until snags and snarls turn the soothing effects into a painful experience. That's where Wahl's Electric Detangling Comb comes to the rescue.

The comb, which looks like a curling iron with eight metal teeth, vibrates and rotates at a speed of 3,000 movements per minute. To use, simply comb as usual. The unit is designed to untangle hair quickly and gently, without irritating your furry friend. And because it vibrates, your pet will enjoy the massaging action as well.

CHAPTER 3

Hardware

It's tool time!

Yes, fixing things that go "boom" in the night has become an American obsession. If you don't believe me, just peruse the aisles of one of those hardware superstores. Loaded on the display racks are thousands of items that promise to make home improvements a snap. In fact twenty years ago if someone suggested that today we would even have hardware superstores, full of nothing but tools, he or she probably would have been committed.

But, as with every major industry featured in this book, new advancements in technology have spurred the growth of the hardware industry to astronomical proportions. Add to that a healthy dose of testosterone and the mainstream popularity of everyone from Bob Vila to Tim Allen to Martha Stewart, and you have the makings of a phenomenon known as the do-it-yourself market.

But enough with my thinking cap, let's put on my hard hat and get to work with the best hardware products of 1997.

HAND TOOLS

Best Value Basic Tools: Craftsman 40-Piece Tool Kit

$150

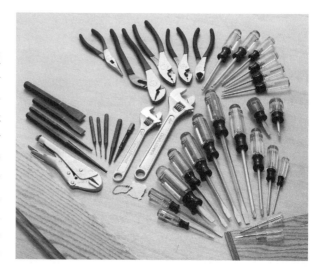

The wrong tool can turn an easy job into a nightmare. That's why it makes sense for any homeowner to purchase an all-purpose tool set, so you're prepared for whatever job might (and will) arise.

For the most durable tools on the market, the Craftsman line-up of tools is the best. This 40-piece set includes 2 adjustable wrenches, 7 pliers, 9-inch V-notch grip pliers, 22 screwdrivers, 2 alignment tools, 5 punches, 2 chisels, and much more.

Best Stud Finder: Zircon

$100

Proving that "high-tech" is not just a buzz-word for the computer generation, Silicon Valley–based Zircon has brought technology to one of the most popular home improvement items of all time—the stud finder. No, this is not a device that will allow you to find me in a crowded room; stud finders are electronic scanning instruments that are invaluable to anyone who has ever tried to hang a picture, locate a faulty wire, or plan a home improvement project. That's because they electronically tell you what's lurking behind the walls before you do any damage. They use a deep-sensing technology and a radarlike readout that pinpoints hidden items up to 6 inches behind walls. Zircon has three models available that have all passed our tests. The StudScanner locates wood or metal studs, the WireScanner locates electrical wiring, and the MetalliScanner finds (you guessed it) metal. A 9-volt battery powers each model.

Best Idea Hand Tool: Deluxe Lite-Driver Kit

$26

Murphy's Law definitely applies to the art of fixing things around the house. If you are like me, then more often than not when there's a screw or nut that needs tightening, it's located in a dark corner or dimly lit crevice. The solution to this dilemma is the Lite Driver. This is a screwdriver that incorporates a flashlight into its design.

Included with the kit is an impact-resistant carrying case that holds 6 interchangeable screw bits (3 flathead, 3 Phillips head) and 6 socket drivers (ranging in size from ³⁄₁₆" to ⁷⁄₁₆", with a nut driver adapter). Embedded in the screwdriver's handle is a tiny spot flashlight positioned to illuminate exactly where your screw is located. It is powered by 2 AA batteries (included) and has an easy on/off switch on its top.

Best Ladder: Telesteps Telescopic Ladder

$260

Every homeowner knows that one of the basic necessities is a good, sturdy ladder. The only problem with most ladders is that they are difficult to store and carry around. And just how do you fit it in the car to get it home from the hardware store in the first place? The Telesteps ladder is the solution. This ladder, when compressed, is only 30 inches tall, but it expands to a whopping 16 feet.

When this ladder was first introduced, I took it on the *Donahue* show, and after Phil was dazzled by its attributes, he decided to climb to the top to see how sturdy it was. The only problem was that the ladder was not leaning against anything—I was the only thing holding it up. So, with me as its steady barrier, Mr. Donahue slowly made the climb, step by step, to the top. As he climbed, the in-house security guards quickly realized what Phil did not—that I was the only thing keeping him alive. Boy, were they waiting for me to fail. But, luckily for Phil, and even luckier for me, I held it up through the end. So take it from me, not only is this ladder compact and easy to use, it is not that difficult to hold up. But don't try this stunt at home.

The Telesteps is definitely the most practical ladder we have ever used. It is made of aluminum and weighs only 23 pounds, but it supports up to 225 pounds. It is important to note that it meets ANSI Type II, Occupational Safety and Health Administration and Canadian safety standards. Its feet are slip-resistant and its top is cushioned to prevent damage to the wall—making it ideal for inside jobs. Each rung features serrated treads for safe climbing and spring-loaded bolts for secure locking. Best of all, opening and closing the Telesteps is a snap and can be easily and quickly done by one person. It is easy to carry too.

POWER TOOLS

Vrroom! There's nothing like the sound of power tools in the morning, and this year's crop have enough features to get even Tim (the toolman Taylor) Allen excited.

Best New Concept Power Tool: Roto Zip SpiraCut Model No. SCS01

$100

Although each year power tool products become more efficient, ergonomic, and easy to use, rarely is there a new category of tool introduced. Breaking this cycle is Roto Zip, a new sawing device that has created its own product niche called Spiral Saws.

Unlike traditional power saws that use a ripping action to cut through materials, the Roto Zip cleanly slices everything from wood and wood laminates to ceramic tile, fiberglass, and drywall. It also has a drill bit attachment and a removable depth-cutting guide for more accuracy.

Powered by a 3.6-amp motor, the secret to this device is its patented interchangeable bits that look like a jigsaw blade but work like a powerful circular saw blade, allowing you to plunge into a work surface easily and begin cutting. It's truly a jigsaw, reciprocating saw, hole saw, and drill all-in-one device.

Other features include an ergonomic handle (with built-in bit storage) for one-handed operation. Its handle can also be removed to convert the unit into a mini-hole drill. It comes with six bit accessories for sawing and drilling and a wrench for bit changes.

Best Multipurpose Power Tool: Dremel

$60

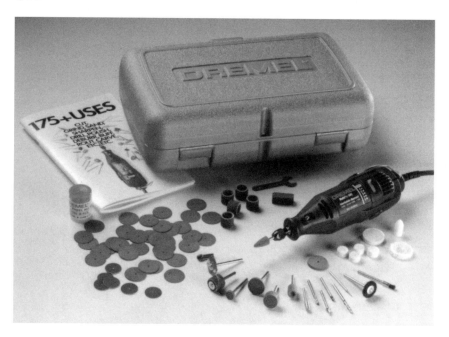

Looking more like something out of your dentist's office than a power tool, the Dremel is quite simply the best little multipurpose tool available.

This versatile handheld power tool comes with more than 125 interchangeable bits that allow you to perform simple tasks like sharpening blades and knives and polishing metals to cutting stripped screwheads off and drilling. For the serious do-it-yourselfer or hobbyist, the Dremel is the perfect companion tool with attachments for wood carving, buffing, routing, and delicate sanding. Its rotating head has five adjustable speeds with an optimal rotation of 30,000 rpm—which is faster than the Road Runner on a good day.

It comes with a hard-shell carrying case and a handy instruction book with more than 175 uses and detailed project descriptions.

Best Cordless Drill: Ryobi Model No. CTH1442K

$165

Whether you're a contractor or a serious do-it-yourselfer, there's nothing worse than using a cordless drill that experiences perennial power problems. Even the easiest of jobs can become a frustrating task when the power keeps shutting off. Ryobi's Model No. CTH1442K is a powerful 14.4-volt cordless drill that delivers more steady power than most rechargeable units, while including all the desirable features such as forward/reverse variable speeds, keyless chuck, and six speed settings.

But what makes this drill different from others is the way it manages its power supply. This rechargeable drill includes two battery packs to provide for nonstop action as well as a new battery recharging system that ensures a perfect charge every time. The charger features built-in diagnostics that constantly read the battery-cell power levels and ambient temperature. This not only promises a full charge every time, but eliminates the possibility of overcharging—which can cut short the life of rechargeable batteries.

Unlike other drills in this category, this one has a soft rubber-type coating on its exterior. This protects the drill from minor drops, and makes it noticeably more comfortable to hold. Because of its near perfectly balanced feel, it is less cumbersome to use on longer, more demanding jobs as well.

TOOLBOXES AND BENCHES

The best way to begin attacking your fix-up projects is with a properly stocked toolbox or home workshop. And because of a wide array of new workshop-oriented products, tackling these chores is not as difficult as it may seem. Probably the number one tool-related headache most of us have is being unable to store all our tools in one convenient location. The result is a hammer here, a screwdriver there, a pair of pliers that is never close at hand when needed. The easiest solution is a toolbox. Unlike the old, heavy metal toolboxes of yesteryear, today's models offer plenty of options.

Best Value Toolbox: Lasko Power Toolbox Model No. 9000
$30

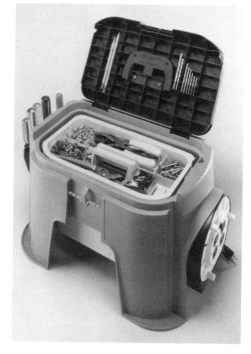

If you operate power tools or floodlights, this toolbox is the best. It not only holds all your stuff, but it also includes a detachable, portable cord reel with a built-in 20-foot extension cord and four 120-volt outlets.

Constructed of a hard plastic resin, its 13½x15½x23½ in. frame can support up to 300 pounds—making it an ideal step stool as well. Its interior features drill bit indentations and pencil clips plus three removable stacking trays with handles that allow you to easi-

ly carry a tray from place to place. Its exterior has molded pockets and holes for larger tools and screwdrivers. It even includes a lock slot for the addition of a padlock to keep your things safe.

Best Multipurpose Toolbox: Black and Decker Shopbox

$46

This portable work center not only holds all your stuff but also features a wooden work surface on its top.

Two front-mounted cranks slide wooden vise jaws, allowing items to be clamped horizontally and vertically. Its work surface measures 18x12 in. and has compartments on its sides for storage. Inside there's a pull-out tray and a deep well for drills and other tools.

Best Value Workbench: Rubbermaid WorkBench Base

$24

The cornerstone to any home workshop is a good workbench, and Rubbermaid recently introduced a kit that allows you to custom-build one to your own specifications.

Called the WorkBench Base, this kit consists of two sturdy plastic sides that allows you to easily and quickly design and make your own workbench. Not included, but required for assembly, is a piece of 4x8x¾ in. plywood (about $15). After sawing the wood into three pieces (for the bottom shelf, backing, and tabletop work surface), you simply attach the pieces to the base (all fasteners are included). Each piece screws directly into the predrilled holes in the workbench sides, and the unit can be fully assembled in less than 30 minutes, yielding a 48x24 in. workbench that can support up to 300 pounds.

Even better, it can be made larger or smaller for a custom fit into just about any workspace.

Best Multipurpose Workbench: Black and Decker Workmate 425

$120

This 31-inch-tall portable project center features a 20x29 in. work surface that can be used as a functional workbench, vise, bench, tool stand, or saw horse.

But what separates this unit from the pack is that although it includes two cranks to secure its vise jaws, you only need to turn one of the cranks to draw the table together. This may not sound earth-shattering, but if you've ever used other two-handed crank vises, you'll definitely appreciate this innovation—especially when one of your hands is holding a piece of wood.

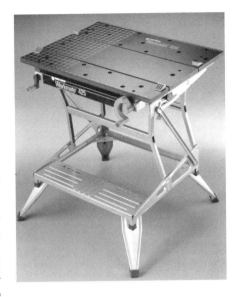

The bench supports up to 550 pounds and its vise holds materials up to 8⅝ inches wide. When you use the unit's swivel pegs, it can hold objects up to 18¾-inches wide. The Workmate folds easily for compact storage and can be hung on a wall when not in use.

Best Benchtop Cutting System: Ryobi BT3000

$550

What makes this 10-inch table saw different from others is that it is expandable—allowing you to start with the basics and add a variety of accessories as your needs and skills grow.

Included in the basic configuration is the 10-inch powered table saw, stand, sliding miter gauge and router plate. You can then add an extension air-flotation table ($100) for larger jobs and connect it to a 28-gallon dust vacuum ($100). This table has a series of tiny holes that, when used in conjunction with the vacuum, automatically draws the accumulated dust into a collection bag. Its airflow can also be reversed to provide an air cushion under larger work pieces, allowing them to easily glide across the surface. This is definitely my favorite of the pack.

YARD AND GARDEN

Whether you have a green thumb or are just all thumbs, the latest trimmers, mowers, mulchers, and sprinklers can help make your outdoor environment the best it can be.

Best Trimmer/Edger: Poulan Weed Eater's Twist 'N' Edge Ultra Trim

$140

The Ultra Trim is a two-cycle gas-powered string trimmer that features a 180-degree twisting shaft that converts the unit from a trimmer to an edger in one easy rotation.

The trimmer head turns from a horizontal to a vertical position with a simple twist of the shaft, allowing for more accurate sidewalk, patio, and flower bed trimming. Other features include a unique no-flood engine mechanism that provides an average first-start rate of 95 percent, meaning you'll spend a lot less time pulling that rip cord.

Best Cordless Hedge Trimmers: Echo Model No. DCH-3000

$400

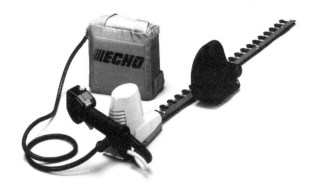

If you want to shape your shrubbery without straining your shoulders, check out the new battery-powered hedge trimmer from Echo.

Powered by an environment-friendly 12-volt battery concealed inside a cushioned backpack, this 30-inch-long, single-sided clipper operates for 5½ hours on an overnight charge. And because you wear the battery pack on your back, the clippers feel lighter (7.2 pounds as opposed to an average 14 pounds for similar, gas-powered units).

Best "Green" Push Mower: Ryobi Mulchinator

$450

When battery-powered mowers first appeared on the market, neighbors cheered them across the world. That's because they are quiet—real quiet. Conservation groups also applauded them as they do not use fossil fuels or emit environmentally unfriendly fumes.

Allow me to note that battery-powered lawn mowers are not for everyone, as a charge only powers the unit for 60 to 90 minutes. But they are ideal for those who only have to mow less than an acre. Or for those who want an excuse to stop mowing.

Our pick of the year, Ryobi's Mulchinator may be the most environment- and neighbor-friendly lawn mower on the market.

This walk-behind model features a 24-volt rechargeable battery that operates for 90 minutes on an overnight charge. And because it is battery-operated, the Mulchinator is quiet and exhaust-free. It's a backsaver too, starting with the flick of a switch, as opposed to the pull of a cord. Because it can be a little too simple to start, a security key is required for activation to keep it safe around children.

Designed for yards of up to one acre, the unit's blade spins fast enough so that it not only cuts your lawn but also mulches the clippings into a chopped natural fertilizer that eliminates the need to bag and dispose of your clippings. This way, you can mow the entire yard without having to stop to empty the bag.

Best Value Riding Mower: Murray Widebody Lawn Tractor $793

Not only is this riding mower a great value at $793, it comes with an exclusive feature called a quick level system that allows you to level your cutting blade, without tools, in less than a minute. This may not sound ground breaking (pun intended), but an unleveled cutting blade is a major headache as it progressively provides a poor, uneven cut to your lawn.

Unlike traditional mowers, which can take several hours and many tools to accurately level the cutting blade, Murray's quick level system allows you to just park your tractor on a flat surface and adjust a switch for a perfectly smooth cut week after week.

It has a 38-inch cutting deck and a 12.5 hp engine. Other features include a six-speed shift-on-the-go transmission, a quick-stall safety switch in the seat that stops the engine should you fall off, and an extra-wide body for more leg room.

Best Use of a Sprinkler: Contech ScareCrow

$100

Are rabbits, birds, and other poachers invading your garden while you sleep? If so, you may want to check out the smartest scarecrow ever invented. Forget the stuffed straw and goofy hat, because this unique sprinkler has a built-in motion sensor that can detect movement in your garden up to 35 feet away in a 100-degree arc. When an intruder is spotted, the ScareCrow releases a powerful blast of water—enough to give even Bugs Bunny a run for his money.

But wait. It gets better. The sprinkler looks just like a scarecrow and doesn't waste much water. The ScareCrow's battery-powered motion sensor only turns the water on for about three seconds, blasting out about two cups. Afterward, the sprinkler sleeps for seven seconds before scanning again. It even makes for a cheap home security device—and promises to soak any burglar that passes through its invisible barrier. The sprinkler can rotate 10 to 360 degrees for normal watering as well. It measures 30 inches tall and weighs 2.4 pounds. This is definitely the first lawn sprinkler that is also a conversation piece!

Best Patio Furniture: Bemis Windsong Sling Chairs and Table

$80 (per chair); $170 (table)

Looks are deceiving when it comes to this patio ensemble. That's because at first glance you would never guess that the chairs and glass-top table were made of a hard plastic resin.

That's because each Sling Chair has a three-position adjustable back and a fabric liner just like more expensive hand-woven patio furniture. But what's best is that unlike its more expensive counterparts, because the furniture is made of plastic, it will never rust, mildew, or stain.

Its round glass-top table pedestal base measures 48 inches in diameter, has an umbrella hole, and weighs 60 pounds (with glass).

Best Do-It-Yourself Book: *The Gadget Guru's Make-It-Easy Guide to Home Repair*

$9.99

Okay, so it's another shameless plug, but this book will actually help you with all those pesky repairs around the house. In it you will find straightforward advice and step-by-step instructions on how to keep plumbing drip-free and flowing, install and repair outlets and other lighting fixtures, hang pictures, do simple carpentry, and even find a professional at a reasonable price, and much more.

CHAPTER 4

Computers

When asked by friends, readers, and viewers if *now's* a good time to buy a computer, I make a comparison to the days when the camcorder industry was in its infancy. During those times I would advise folks that they could bet that camcorders will be better, include more features, and cost less the following year. But if they put off the purchase, just think how many memories would be missed. With computers, it's the same.

Yes, it's a safe bet that next year you will be able to purchase a computer that is faster, loaded with more features, and less expensive than current models. But if there are things you could be doing on a computer today, you should buy one now.

The computer industry has developed into a dysfunctional family of sorts. The manufacturers have developed an appliance that has become a commodity, but have failed at making it foolproof.

Yes, computers are not perfect. They can crash, are not compatible with many of the add-on peripherals they are designed to work with, and can be complicated to set up and use. Reliability has not progressed at the same pace as the advancement of the circuitry that allows them to process information. It has come to the point that most users require a friendship with someone who can drop over and repair or reconfigure the computer on a moment's notice; in my circle of friends his name is Rob. I know this makes it sound as if I'm not a fan of computers, but I am. They have improved our lives immeasurably.

Computers give parents a new method of educating even the youngest of children. They are necessary for the student and have become the hobby of choice among senior citizens. When my father was looking for a new hobby, I got him a computer. Although it's safe to say that he is not a technological wizard, I knew that once he leaped the technophobe hurdle, using a computer was a hobby he would surely sink his teeth into. And he did. He is now a computer lover and uses his Macintosh on a daily basis. From writing letters to checking financial information to sending e-mail to his grandchildren, the computer has changed his life—for the better! He has become so fond of his own technological revolution that he now maintains a full home-office setup and can do just about anything there that I can do in my own professional office.

Why did I buy him a Macintosh? To preserve my sanity, that's why. Although the Macintosh is slowly slipping into oblivion and hanging on to dear life by its fingernails, it still uses the simplest operating system in the world. Macintosh perfected the point-and-click interface and has made the computer a home appliance because of it. But the Macintosh has turned into such a small factor of the industry that it is not taken seriously anymore. In fact, many wonder how much longer Apple can stay in business. But allow me to state that if you are seeking to enter the world of computers, and are fearful of the experience, the Macintosh is definitely the way to go. Yes, there is not as much software available for a Mac as there are for its Windows counterparts, but I dare you to find an application where there is no Macintosh software solution. The assortment may be smaller, but there are software titles that can meet any need.

That stated, there is a lesson to be learned by the computer manufacturers and software publishers (are you listening, Bill Gates?) of the world from the consumer electronics industry—and that's *keep it simple* and *make them reliable.*

Just imagine if your television or telephone worked with the same reliability as a computer. What would you do when you changed channels and received a message such as "This channel has performed an illegal operation and will be shut down"? Or how about a telephone that did not give you a dial tone every time you picked up the handset? How long would it take for you to start screaming at the top of your lungs that you are mad as hell and not going to take it anymore? Not long, I guarantee it! How many times do you call the cable company when the service drops out? Well if you try to do that to a computer manufacturer, you will be stuck in voice-mail hell—that is unless you want to call its 900 number and pay to find out how to fix the problem. Yes, the computer industry is the unruly teenager—and as we learn how to live with him or her, we know that as the teen matures, he or she will grow into a respectable, responsible individual.

This chapter is a mature look at the PC industry. In it you will not only find advice on how and what PC and printer to buy, but the best accessories and software for the home and home office that promise to make computing not only easier, but also fun.

As a special bonus, because the computer industry and the products generated from it constantly change, and book deadlines don't, we, together with the great editorial staff from Warner Books, have decided to make this a virtual chapter. This means that this chapter will be constantly updated in cyberspace. Although this chapter will show you the basics of the best products of the year, you will be able to go to my Web site and see even more new computer news.

You may ask: If I'm reading this chapter to find out which computer is right for me, and I have to go to the Internet to see the updated information, how do I do it if I don't have a computer?

The answer is simple. These days everyone knows someone who uses a computer to go online. Just grab a nice bottle of wine and nicely ask them if they will surf you to the site. To get there, just go to http://www.gadgetguru.com and click on the listing Best Book. That will take you to the right place. But there's more. At the bottom of the page, there is a box that requires a password to see the updated information. This takes you to an area reserved solely for book buyers—not those wanting a free ride! The password is *Book* and the user name is *Best.* There is an area there that will allow you to send e-mail messages to my staff for questions, comments, or opinions of this book. Have fun!

In the meantime here are our picks for 1997, and a quick primer that promises to make you sound so much like a pro, you'll scare the salesperson into telling you the truth.

COMPUTER TECHNOBABBLE:
A QUICK GLOSSARY

- **RAM:** An acronym for random-access memory. Your computer has two ways of storing data: the hard drive (see below), and internal memory (RAM). A computer takes data and sends it into RAM for temporary storage. More RAM translates into quicker, more seamless processing. It allows the computer to quickly process—that translates into smooth computing. **Buying tip:** New computer buyers should look for models with at least 16 MB of RAM. However, the more RAM the merrier. If you can afford it, look for models that boast 24 MB or even 32 MB of memory. You will truly see a difference.

- **MHz:** An abbreviation for megahertz. It's the clock speed of the microprocessor (the computer's brain). The higher the number, the faster the information is processed. The number of MHz relates to how many millions of instructions can be processed per second. **Buying tip:** Shop for units with at least 133 MHz. The higher the number the better.

- **MMX:** An acronym for MultiMedia Extension. It is Intel's (maker of the Pentium chip) first new chip in ten years. MMX is an enhancement chip optimized for multimedia CD-ROMs and imaging. MMX chips are currently available in 166 MHz and 200 MHz microprocessors. The MMX chip allows for more efficient and speedy processing (20 percent faster for existing applications and 60 percent faster for MMX-enhanced software). MMX machines add about $200 to $300 to the cost of a computer, as compared to their Pentium counterparts.

- **Modem:** An acronym for modulator/demodulator. Simply stated, it is the device that connects a computer to a phone line so that information can be sent from one computer to another. It's necessary for gaining access to an online service or the Internet. **Buying tip:** It will be difficult to find a computer that does not have at least a 33.6 kbps (kilobits per second) modem. Be on the lookout for 56 kbps upgrades and cable modems that will allow you to connect it to your television cable for lightning-fast speeds.

- **PCMCIA:** An acronym for personal computer miniature communications interface (jokingly known as "people can't make clear, intuitive acronyms"). It's a memory and modem card, about the size of a credit card, which connects to your PC or laptop. PCM-CIA cards are generally used as modems for laptop communications but have other uses such as memory functions.

- **Hard Drive:** The hard drive is like your computer's filing cabinet, and just like real filing cabinets the more you have, the more space you can fill up. **Buying tip:** Look for units with at least one gigabyte (GB) hard drive.

- **CD-ROM:** An acronym for compact disc read-only memory. Standard on all computers, CD-ROM drives allow you to load software, and play music CDs and games on your PC. CD-ROM drives have different speeds. Today's standard is an 8X speed CD-ROM, but some deliver up to 16X. The higher the speed the faster the disc spins, making data read faster from its laser.

- **DVD-ROM:** An acronym for digital versatile disc read-only memory. These devices are promising to be the next big thing in PCs and have started appearing on computers this year. Please note that DVD-ROM drives also play CD-ROMs, but CD-ROM drives do not play DVD-ROMs. Like its consumer electronics cousin (see chapter 1), DVD-ROMs will revolutionize the way we play and work on the PC. The reason is simple. DVD-ROMs have a much larger storage capacity than CD-ROMs and are designed to play full-motion video in a super-high–quality mode. Hence, they are a software developer's dream as more graphics and more information can be packed on one disc. Even better, you will be able to play DVD movie software on your computer's DVD-ROM drive. However, DVD-ROMs will not currently play on DVD home theater players. The DVD will be playing a major role in the marriage between the television and the computer. **Buying tip:** DVD-ROM software titles will be scarce until next year, and with the possibility of recordable DVDs on the horizon, my advice is to wait before upgrading your existing PC to a DVD-ROM drive to see how this technology shakes out. However, when shopping, if you can afford it, a DVD-ROM player is a good investment.

DESKTOPS

When you stop and think about it, aside from your home and possibly your car, a personal computer is probably one of the most difficult albeit important purchasing decisions you can make.

To further confuse the issue, this year's crop of desktop computers run the gamut from great value entry-level units to more user-defined imaging, business, and gamer PCs. That's why it is important to know what you are looking for before you enter the marketplace.

Best Value Computer: Monorail

$800

Proving the fact that electronic products get better and less expensive each year, you can now purchase a full-function, although not necessarily the fastest, computer for under a thousand dollars. The Monorail PC is a sleekly designed desktop computer that truly packs a lot of bang for the buck. In fact, the folks at Monorail can be credited for lighting a fire under the feet of the major manufacturers and motivating them to address the budget-conscious consumer with lower priced, value-oriented products.

Designed for the first-time buyer, this charcoal-colored desktop computer consumes only about 20 percent of the desk space of its larger counterparts. It features a 10.4-inch flat-panel color screen (with larger sizes available by the end of the year), 16 MB of RAM (expandable to 80 MB), a 1 GB hard drive, and is powered by a 75 MHz microprocessor that is upgradable to a 133 MHz or 200 MHz microprocessor.

The Monorail's standard configuration includes a 33.6 kbps modem, a 4X CD-ROM drive, a floppy disk drive, a 16-bit Sound Blaster–compatible audio system, and built-in stereo speakers. A full-size keyboard, mouse, and a microphone are included as well. All the cables are color-coded for easy connection, which enables users to get the computer up and running in a matter of minutes. Also included are game and video ports on the back of the unit for connecting joysticks and an external video monitor.

What's even better is Monorail's service. In an agreement with Federal Express, any time the Monorail PC needs to be upgraded or serviced, users can simply ship the unit in its original box to the manufacturer via FedEx and receive it back within seven business days. That can be easier than lugging it back and forth to the place of purchase.

The Monorail PC comes loaded with Windows 95 and Internet Explorer.

Best Value Full-Size Desktop: Compaq Presario No. 2200

$800
(without monitor)

Another best value in the under $1,000 price range is Compaq's Presario 2200.

At first glance, this unit looks different from other low-cost units: it's smaller, sized more like a VCR than a computer, and it's colored black to give it a high-tech, stylish look.

Included in this model is a 180 MHz Cyrix (not Intel Pentium) microprocessor, 16 MB of RAM, a 1.6 GB hard drive, an 8X CD-ROM drive, and a 33.6 (upgradable to 56 kbps) modem. Other features include two built-in speakers, and like other Compaq models, it will feature sleep and volume buttons on its front panel.

It comes loaded with Windows 95, Microsoft Works, Compton's 1997 Encyclopedia, Amazon Trail, Quicken SE, Pinball, and online services. A monitor is not included, but Compaq is offering a matching 14-inch color monitor at a great value price of $200. It is also important to understand that this unit is designed for home users, not for those needing to connect to an office network, as no expansion slots are included.

Best Apple Computer: Home Series PowerMac 6500

$2,500 (without monitor)

When Microsoft first unveiled its Windows 95 operating system in August 1995, some creative Macintosh fan developed a bumper sticker that said Windows 95 = Apple 89. While that's not entirely true, it does hold some validity when it comes to ease of use. Although Microsoft has been  trying for years to come up with operating systems as easy to use as the Macintosh, they still haven't been able to catch up. That's the good news for Apple. The bad news is that Microsoft has gotten so far ahead on the bell curve when it comes to software and performance that the Apple seems like it is stuck living in its own mythical world where every day is 1989.

However, there is hope as Apple's founder, Steve Jobs, has returned and a new operating system code named Rhapsody is on the way in 1998, which is based on Jobs's NeXt (brand name) technology.

That said, Apple still makes the easiest-to-use computers on the planet. The Macintosh is also the computer of choice for graphic designers who have learned that its interface is quicker than its Windows counterparts.

Although there are fewer software titles for Macs than there are for Windows computers, there are some surprises—such as Quicken (see page 181). While most software companies develop software primarily for Windows computers, and might come up with a rewritten Mac version, the latest version of Quicken is more intuitive and easier to use than its Windows counterpart. It also knocks the socks off other home and small-business checking/financial programs.

The bottom line is that if you fear technology, buy a Mac—it will turn you into a computer lover!

The best Apple is the Home Macintosh PowerMac 6500. This unit includes a super-fast 300 MHz power PC processor, 64 MB of RAM, a 6-gigabyte hard drive, a 56 kbps modem and a 12X CD-ROM player plus a built-in Zip drive, which increases a hard drive's storage capacity. In addition, all new Macintosh computers will read most Windows and DOS files.

Best Value Step-Up Computer: Compaq Presario No. 4504

$999 (without monitor)

Two years ago a personal computer that included a Pentium 166 MHz processor cost upwards of $2,500 and was considered state of the art. Quite frankly, although a Pentium 200 MHz-based computer is not state of the art, it is still a great system for just about anyone. The good news is that now you can buy a 200 MHz computer for under $1,000. (Isn't technology great?)

Designed to compete respectably in a price war, Compaq's Presario No. 4504 includes a 200 MHz Pentium processor, 16 MB of RAM, a 2.1 GB hard drive, a 16X CD-ROM, and a 33.6 kbps modem. Simply stated, this is a great bang-for-the-buck computer.

Best Family Imaging Computer: Hewlett-Packard Pavilion 7350P

$1,400 (without monitor)

As mentioned earlier, one of the hottest technologies to hit the PC marketplace is the proliferation of digital cameras and photo-quality printers. To perform these tasks, the brains and the brawn have to come from the PC, and Hewlet-Packard's real-life imaging computer is just the ticket.

This 166 MHz MMX-enhanced PC comes with software programs that include easy-to-use tools, graphic images and photos, plus imaging hardware like a built-in Zip drive for storing images and a scanner that allow you to insert photographs into your PC.

The 7350P's color scanner is built into its mini-tower and allows you to scan photos up to 5x7 directly into the PC. In addition to its 1.44 MB floppy disk drive there's also a built-in Zip drive that lets you store 100 MB of information or graphics on a single disk. The Zip drive works just like your PC's hard drive, giving you quick access to anything you've stored, without eating up valuable hard disk space. This is ideal for storing photographs and graphic images as they can quickly deplete even the largest of hard disk drives.

Other features include a telephone answering machine and a unique keyboard with "hot buttons" for one-touch access to the Internet or your favorite software applications, as well as the controls for the CD-ROM and volume (two 16-bit speakers and a built-in sound card are included). It has a 2.5 GB hard drive, 32 MB of RAM, a 33.6 kbps modem, 16X CD-ROM and video inputs on its back panel for videophones and for transferring video from your VCR or camcorder into the computer.

Best-Features Family Computer: Gateway P5-200

$2,500

If you want the latest in PC technology that not only satisfies all your home-office and family needs but also knocks your socks off with MMX-enhanced multimedia game play, look no further than this unit from Gateway 2000.

Featuring a 200 MHz MMX Pentium processor, a 12X speed CD-ROM drive, 32 MB of RAM, a 2.5 GB hard drive, and a top-quality sound card with 16-bit Altec Lansing speakers with Dolby Pro Logic playback capabilities (see stereos, chapter 1) and subwoofer, Gateway delivers the goods.

The computer comes bundled with Microsoft Office 97 and five MMX-enhanced software titles and includes a 17-inch color monitor in its $2,500 price.

Allow me to note that Gateway is a mail-order only company and its models are not found in stores. But its Mom and Pop reputation has made it one of the most reliable and customer service–friendly companies in the industry today.

Best Gamer Computer: AST Gamer PC

$2,299 (without monitor)

If you prefer Air Warrior to Quicken, Indy Car Racing to word processing, or a round of golf at Augusta National to spreadsheets, then the latest AST computer, optimized for the hard-core gamer, is the best in the business.

Of course this PC will perform all your financial and family functions but where it really makes the grade is with its multimedia-enhanced configuration. Featuring a Pentium 233 MHz MMX processor, 32 MB of RAM, a whopping 5 GB hard disk drive, a 24X CD-ROM, and 56 kbps modem, this PC is ready for the races.

This MMX PC will perform up to 60 percent faster than its Pentium counterparts so with the new generation of MMX-enhanced games hitting shelves you will be a participant not a spectator.

Other features include 2 MB of video memory, an included game pad with joystick, a 3-D video card with graphics acceleration, and two powerful speakers and subwoofer.

Best Office Computer: Hewlett-Packard Vectra 500

$2,200

Although the aforementioned units are great for the home and some business applications, they might not meet the needs of many small or larger offices. Businesses today do not need computers loaded with games and other software packages. They require computers that are extremely reliable and can be configured for multiple applications. That's the niche that HP's Vectra series fits into.

Instead of being sold in standard discount or retail stores, they are sold at VARs (value added retailers). These are servicing dealers that specialize in configuring computers for specific tasks. In fact, I am writing this book on a Vectra 500 and have found it to be extremely reliable—so much so that I consider it bulletproof! This model is available in a variety of configurations including the graphic-friendly MMX processors. What it did not include though was a modem, a network card, a sound card, and speakers. That's because some offices need them and some don't. Why pay for something you won't need? It has 166 MHz MMX with 32 MB of memory and a 1.6 GB hard disk drive.

LAPTOPS

Although it was not always this way, today's notebook computers have become just as powerful as their desktop counterparts. However, not all notebook computers are created equal. Characteristically, notebooks cost more than desktops and some are so overpriced you'd think you were buying a NASA workstation instead of a portable computer. Remember, the trick to buying is recognizing your specific needs and desires.

- For travelers, make sure the laptop weighs seven pounds or less. After trudging with these things through O'Hare or LAX airport a few times, believe me, you will be wishing for the old days of pencils and graph paper. **Tip:** If your laptop has interchangeable floppy disk and CD-ROM drives, load all your software before you travel and leave the drives at home. This will drop a few pounds from your laptop and make it easier to transport.

- If you are buying a notebook computer that will be used primarily at home or in a dorm room, and only occasionally on the road, look for one with a comfortable keyboard and a large screen. You may even want to consider connecting an auxiliary monitor or keyboard for more user comfort. **Tip:** A 12.1-inch screen should be the minimum size for a laptop. Although larger screens can translate into bulkier, heavier computers, they are easier on the eyes. Our testing has shown that NEC, Sharp, Apple, and IBM make the best screens.

- Laptops generally come with two different modem options: an internal modem or a PCMCIA card (see pages 148–149) that connects to a slot in the laptop. Check this out before you buy, as a modem is often a necessity in a notebook computer. **Tip:** Modems are options on some laptops, so ask the salesman if a modem is included. If you plan on sending/receiving e-mail, faxes, and other communications via your laptop, look for an internal or PCMCIA with a minimum modem speed of 33.6 kbps. PCMCIA cards cost about $200. Internal modems are less expensive. Remember, it's easier to upgrade a PCMCIA card than it is an internal modem.

• Test the mouse-tracking device before buying. Laptops have a variety of different pointer options such as mini trackballs, tiny eraser-sized devices located on the keyboard, and flat touch screens. **Tip:** No two mouse track devices are alike. Choose the one you are most comfortable with because there's nothing worse than a temperamental mouse. Try it before you buy it.

• Make sure there is ample room below the keyboard for your wrist. Cramping is a major problem with some of the less ergonomic notebooks.

Best No-Frills Value Laptop: Compaq Armada

$1,300

If you want a good laptop that won't break your budget, check out this best value unit from Compaq.

No, it doesn't offer all the bells and whistles of its higher-priced counterparts. But yes, it includes enough stuff to keep you mobile, including a 120 MHz Pentium processor, 16 MB of RAM, an internal floppy disk drive, and a 1.08 GB hard drive.

It includes a small but functional 10.1-inch screen, a full-sized keyboard and palm rest, and it weighs in at a respectable 6.1 pounds. What it doesn't have is a CD-ROM drive or a modem (it does have two PCM-CIA card slots)—but hey, if you need either one, you'll have plenty of dough left over to go out and buy it.

Best Laptop: IBM ThinkPad 560

$2,700+

For the frequent traveler or the businessperson on the go, the innovation in a notebook award goes to IBM for its ThinkPad 560. This ultra thin (1.2-inch-thick) unit weighs a mere 4.1 pounds and has become my notebook travel companion of choice. It is available in a variety of Pentium configurations, starting in price at $2,700.

Besides its impressive size and weight, this laptop is loaded with lots of other features. These include an extra-large 12.1-inch display (rumored to leap to 13.1 inches by the time this book goes on sale—so check our Web site), an ergonomic wrist rest, and an innovative, easy-to-navigate track-point mouse control located between the G and H keys on the keyboard. I honestly cannot say enough good things about this model.

Best Laptop for Your Desktop: NEC Versa 6200MX

$6,400

What distinguishes this computer from other notebooks is its display screen. Bar none, this 13.3-inch screen is the clearest and easiest to read on the market today.

It includes a 166 MHz MMX-enhanced Pentium processor, 32 MB of RAM, a 3 GB hard drive, and two PCMCIA card slots. Also included are a 10X CD-ROM and a floppy disk drive. These two drives are inter-changeable and slide in and out of the unit as needed.

Although NEC says it weighs 7 pounds it feels much heavier, that's why I wouldn't recommend this unit to the frequent traveler. It's great as a home or dorm room desktop replacement, or for occasional travelers. Other features include integrated speakers as well as a microphone. It comes bundled with 15 software titles.

Best Apple Laptop: PowerBook 3400c/240

$3,500

This is the best laptop from Apple in years! This powerful portable packs an impressive 240MHz power PC processor, a 12.1-inch screen, and of course Apple's most acclaimed feature: the easiest-to-use operating system on the market.

Other features include 16 MB of RAM, a 33.6 kbps modem with Ethernet built in for office networking (a great feature when you need to work with an office network), a whopping 3 GB hard drive, and interchangeable floppy and 16X CD-ROM drives. For presentations in the office or on the road, the PowerBook features a 16-bit video-out/video-in capability plus a unique four-speaker sound system. It has two PCMCIA card expansion bays and weighs a respectable 7.2 pounds.

Best Laptop for the Rugged Individualist (Tie): Panasonic CF-25MK II and FieldWorks FW5000 WorkStation

$4,800 (Panasonic); $5,000 (FieldWorks)

There's just one thing a notebook computer cannot do—bounce. Yes, that expensive high-tech investment is always just a few feet from destruction. And no warranty in the world is going to cover an accidental drop from the desktop to the floor. But there's a growing category of ruggedized laptops designed to "take a licking and keep on ticking." These units can withstand falls, rain, and even liquid spillage, protecting your notebook computer from all of life's little mishaps.

Panasonic's CF-25 features a shock-resistant magnesium alloy exterior that is 20 times stronger than the ABS plastic found on most laptops. But don't let its tough exterior fool you, the CF-25 weighs a respectable 7 pounds (with battery) and measures 2⅓x11⁷⁄₁₀x9⅓ in. Because all of its components are water-resistant, this laptop can withstand exposure to rain or spillage without any internal or external damage.

The CF-25's hard disk and floppy drives are mounted in a vibration-absorbing material that reduces impact to less than one-third of conventional mountings.

Its 12.1-inch color screen features a nonglare display for acceptable viewing both indoors and out and is securely attached to the magnesium frame in 12 places, so that it can survive bumps and falls from as high as 30 inches onto a concrete surface.

In terms of power, the CF-25 includes 16 MB of RAM and offers a 150 MHz Pentium processor and 2 GB hard drive. It includes two

PCMCIA card slots and a built-in floppy disk drive. An optional 10X speed CD-ROM drive is also available.

FieldWorks FW5000 WorkStation is also considered a virtually indestructible notebook computer. Sized just slightly larger (3½x12½x13 in.) and heavier (10 pounds) than the aforementioned unit, this model features a rubberized magnesium-alloy frame that claims to be 20 times stronger than a regular laptop. Inside, its components are shock-mounted for safety and sealed for protection against accidental spills. Not only can you drop the WorkStation from an eight-story building, the company also guarantees that you can even run it through the dishwasher without losing a byte of data. It can withstand temperatures ranging from below zero to above 100 degrees, as well as withstand up to 100 Gs of force.

On the functional side, its standard configuration includes a 100 MHz Pentium processor, 8 MB of RAM, a 810 MB hard drive, two PCMCIA slots, and stereo speakers. The modem is not included.

Four expansion bays are also included, and two of them can handle an additional floppy and/or CD-ROM drive.

PRINTERS

Like Abbot and Costello, Ben and Jerry, or Katie and Matt, a personal computer and printer are meant to go together.

Once you've determined it's time to purchase a new or replacement printer, here's the first decision you need to make: ink-jet or laser? If all you do is print text, and don't mind spending a bit more money, a laser printer is your best bet. But if color copies are part of your agenda, an ink-jet is the printer for you. This year is highlighted by the introduction of true photo-quality ink-jet printers. Never mind the "near photo-quality" and "almost photo-quality" jargon from previous years, the current offerings could have you bypassing the corner photo store when you are in need of a reprint. In fact, the latest generations of printers are so strong, the folks at Kodak are surely suffering sleepless nights.

But creating photo-quality prints is expensive. To achieve this, you first have to either purchase a scanner, a digital camera, or have your film transferred to a photo CD so that the images can be read by your computer. Although you can print on normal paper, special photo paper that costs about $1 a sheet is required for printing higher-quality images. And don't forget those ink-jet refills, which can cost upwards of $40. So before you buy, check and see the cost of refills.

The evolution of printers is nothing short of amazing. In 1997 you can buy a photo-quality printer for under $400 or a laser printer for as low as $300. Ten years ago when I first started my business I purchased a laser printer for more than $4,000. Although it was top-of-the-line then, it is now an antique.

PRINTER TECHNOSPEAK

- **DPI:** Dots per inch. A measurement term that refers to how many ink dots fit into a horizontal and vertical grid of one square inch. In general, the higher the dpi the better. For example, 600x600 dpi means 360,000 dots can be placed within a square inch on the printed page. But be wary of dpi manipulation, such as companies claiming that 360x360 dpi is 720 dpi. **Tip:** For home or small offices, look for printers with a minimum of 600x600 dpi for both black and color printing needs. However, some companies are now touting higher resolution rates of up to 1440x720.

   Although not every retailer will let you do this, a good way to beat the confusion is to take an image on a photo CD to a store and ask for a demo. Seeing is believing.

- **PPM:** Pages per minute. This rating shows how fast a printer can produce average documents. **Tip:** As a rule, text prints faster than color, and lasers are faster than ink-jets. But there are exceptions.

- **Ink-jet** or **bubble jet:** A type of color printer that uses sealed cartridges to contain the ink. They spray microscopic streams of ink onto the page to form letters or graphics.

- **Laser:** A type of printer that uses heat and a laser beam to print. In general lasers are faster with speeds up to 8 PPM. But that too is changing. Unlike ink-jet cartridges, lasers use a more economical toner cartridge, which costs about $40 and needs replacing around every 1,000 pages. Consumer lasers (those under

$1,000) print only in black-and-white, so they are best for the small office/home office (SOHO) with no color needs.

• **Cartridges:** These are the small plastic ink containers that have individual reservoirs for each ink color. **Tip:** Many low-cost ink-jet printers use three-color ink-jets to print the black text as well as color. This depletes the cartridge much faster and replacement cost or refills can be expensive. For heavy use, look for printers that either enable you to insert two separate cartridges (black and color) or have an additional four-color cartridge adding the black well inside. Heavy text users should opt for models that allow larger black ink cartridges.

➤ **And remember:** Printers do not come with printer cables. Don't leave the store without cable to connect the printer to your PC—this will result in an immediate U-turn back to the store. Printer cables sell for around $8.

Best Value Ink-Jet Printer: Epson 400

$200

Don't let its low price fool you, Epson has delivered a winner with this model. This four-color ink-jet printer is great for the home or as a color companion to the office's laser printer.

It prints black text and color images at 720x720 dpi. On the text side, this is better than many laser printers. It delivers text pages at 4 PPM and can deliver color images as fast as 2 PPM—depending on the size of the image.

It is simple to use as it comes with an easy-to-install driver/CD-ROM with troubleshooting capabilities and an on-screen "gas gauge" that displays the level of ink remaining in the cartridges. Also included with this printer is an excellent software package that contains Sierra Print Artist and Adobe Photo Deluxe as well as extra fonts, art images, and high-resolution photos.

Best Output Photo-Quality Ink-Jet Printer:
Epson Stylus Color 600
(Runner-Up: Lexmark 7000)

$500 (Epson);
$400 (Lexmark)

Giving photomats a run for their money is the Epson Stylus. After testing, all I can say is that if you're into imaging, buy this photo printer. It's truly remarkable. It features a six-color ink-jet cartridge and is PC and Mac compatible from the start.

For photo and text quality in the small or home office the Epson Stylus 800 ($450) adds a faster engine speed with an 8 PPM speed (the fastest in the industry), networking capabilities, plus an Adobe post script option for higher-quality printouts.

The runner-up is Lexmark's 7000. This model delivers a whopping 1,200x1,200 dpi, a text print speed of 8 PPM (in water- and smear-proof ink), and an on-screen gas gauge that shows how much ink is remaining. It delivers top-quality color output that rivals higher-priced dedicated photo printers. Also included is Live Pix software— an image-processing program that allows you to manipulate images and, unlike other similar programs, is simple to use. It retails for $400.

Allow me to note that at press time Canon had not yet finalized the details on its photo-quality printer. However, by the looks of the print samples they sent over, expect to see excellent photo-quality units from them as well. Canon also revealed that its hot printer this year will not only print, but convert into a color scanner with an attachment that replaces the ink-jet cartridge. Of course by the time this book is released I'll be reviewing everything, so you can get the latest information on our Web site (see beginning of chapter 4).

Best Photo System for the Home: Hewlett-Packard PhotoSmart Photo Printer and PhotoSmart Photo Scanner

$500 each

Opening the door to a whole new category of photo processing on the PC, Hewlett-Packard's photo printer device and companion photo scanner are making it easier and more affordable for consumers to enter the exciting world of imaging at home.

The PhotoSmart Printer is the first ink-jet printer for the home to use six ink colors and multiple saturation levels to produce professional-quality photographs. Allow me to note that although this is an ink-jet printer, unlike the other models on the market, it is not designed for heavy text use. But for those looking for a printer to process photographic images at home, this one is the best on the market. In fact, when I showed this one on the *Today* show, our staff was hard-pressed to identify which photo came from the professional processor and which was made on this printer. It really is that good.

In terms of the printer, it features a straight paper path that allows you to use thicker photo papers for prints that are suitable for framing and, something you'll probably never use: good, better, and best print modes. After all, if you are buying this printer for pure photo-quality printing at home, why would you want to use the good or better mode?

Costwise, each color print with paper and ink will cost you around $2/per 8x10 in best print mode while smaller prints will be a bit less. When you compare this to a photo retailer that would charge upwards of $7 to convert a negative to an 8x10 image, this is truly a bargain. The unit comes with two cartridges (both are required) and replacements sell for $40 each—or a total of two for $80.

Because this model is geared specifically for photos, it truly delivers quality prints from your PC. Those wanting to set up an easy-to-use photo center at home should consider the additional purchase of HP's PhotoSmart scanner. This is the easiest to operate scanner I have ever tested. To use, just press a button designating what type of original you are starting with: photo, negative, or slide. Then just insert the desired original and watch, while a thumbnail version of the image appears on the screen. Then just tell it what size image you would like printed and, voilà! printing commences. The scanner accepts photos up to 5x7 in. and allows you to print the same size as the original, wallet-size, or up to 8x10 in. HP's PhotoSmart scanner is ideal for home or home-office use and is the perfect companion to its PhotoSmart printer.

Best Idea Photo Printer: Lexmark Color Jet Printer Model No. 7205

Around $500

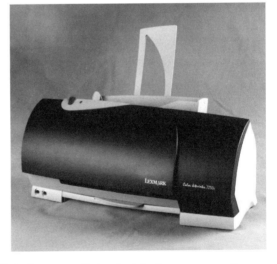

It's a safe bet that most computer owners also have a camcorder lying around the house as well. But, did you know the resolution of camcorder images is many times better than the latest crop of digital cameras? And with the proper software you can transmit still images from your camcorder to the PC and print them out just like other media. Until now, that process was cumbersome as you needed extra cables and special devices to perform camcorder-to-PC-to-printer functions.

To the rescue comes Lexmark with the world's first printer with audio/video hookups on its front panel. This allows you to connect your camcorder easily to your printer with the same jacks that connect to your TV. Combined with its included software package, you can create high-quality digital snapshots from your camcorder footage and print them on your printer.

The ink-jet printer prints 1,200x1,200 dpi and is great for just text printing too, as it has a dedicated black cartridge that fits next to its three-color cartridge. It prints at a fast 8 PPM and best of all sells for under $500.

Best SOHO Ink-Jet Printer: Canon BJC-4550

$500

What makes this printer noteworthy is that it is the first ink-jet printer that not only prints on standard 8½x11 in. paper but on 11x17 in. paper as well. Combine this with its under $500 price, and this becomes a desirable product for the SOHO market.

Unlike standard 8½x11-inch printers, this product makes it simple to compose and print newsletters, catalogs, and larger brochures without needing to use professional printing services. Even better, unlike most printers that are either Macintosh or Windows compatible, this printer works with both operating systems.

Sized 8½x17½x10 in., it is not much larger than standard ink-jet printers and easily fits on a desktop. It delivers a 360-dpi print quality and prints text at a speed of 5 PPM and color graphics at 1 PPM. Also included is an automatic sheet feeder that holds up to 100 standard-sized or 50 ledger-sized pages or 15 envelopes.

Best Value Laser Printer: Okidata 4w

$300

For the best value and best-sized laser printer on the market look no further than this unit from Okidata.

Compatible with Windows operating systems, it delivers a crisp 600 dpi black-and-white print quality and includes a 100-sheet paper tray. It's small too, measuring only 6x12¼x7½ in., making this printer's footprint the same size as a piece of paper. This little laser prints 4 PPM at 600x600 dpi and handles a wide variety of paper types from envelopes to overhead projection transparencies. The toner cartridge lasts for 1,000 pages and replacements sell for $28.

Best Home-Office Laser Printer: Brother HL-730DX

$400

Another great value in a laser is this unit from Brother. This unit prints black-and-white text at 600x600 dpi at a fast 6 PPM and has a 200-sheet paper tray. The toner cartridge lasts for 2,200 pages and replacements sell for $34.

As a bonus, if you've become frustrated trying to print Web

sites in a presentation or brochure, you'll appreciate Brother's inclusion of a software package called Surf and Print, which allows you to automatically turn Internet files into printed booklets for easy archiving and presentations. This Brother model is available for both Windows and Macintosh operating systems.

Best Multifunction Machine: Canon MultiPass C-3000

$600

For the home or small office, one of the best products on the market is the new generation of multifunction machines. These units combine several tasks into one handy unit. Our favorite multifunction is the Canon MultiPass.

This unit consolidates bubble jet color printing, plain-paper faxing, monochrome scanning, copying, and PC fax capabilities all in one product. It offers 720x360 dpi, true four-color printing on a variety of media as well as up to 5 PPM monochrome printing. The plain-paper fax function offers similar features to those found on Canon's stand-alone facsimile machines, including battery backup and one-touch faxing. Multitasking is made possible by a 24-page memory that can store incoming messages while the unit is performing printing or copying functions.

The MultiPass C3000 also provides copying with quality-enhanced 360 dpi. The 20-page automatic document feeder also helps to save time and allows for multiple copies. The 400-dpi monochrome scanner gives home professionals and their families the ability to scan text, logos, and line art into their PC, adding a personal touch to graphics or text documents. Scanning documents into the PC for electronic storage can also reduce clutter in the home office. You can direct the various functions of the MultiPass C3000 easily through Canon's software that includes a full-featured PC fax.

Best Portable Printer: Citizen PN60i

$500

For those of us (like me) who spend more time in hotel rooms than our own homes, portable printers have become a real life-saver—especially when trying to meet a deadline while on the road.

This ink-jet printer is ideal for small print jobs, occasional usage, or when trying to put together a boardroom-quality presentation while away from the office. Weighing just 1.1 pounds and small enough (2x10x1⅝ in.) to fit in a briefcase, this unit is sized more like a roll of aluminum foil than a printer.

It includes a black mini-cassette cartridge that prints 30 pages of text at 2 PPM and can be interchanged with an optional color cartridge that prints 3 to 5 PPM. Replacement cartridges are sold as two-packs and cost $10 for the black and $15 for color. The PN60i can be used with envelopes and transparencies as well as with standard paper.

Also included is infrared data capability so you can wirelessly beam your data from any IRDA-compatible laptop computer or PDA to the printer.

It includes an AC adapter and can be used with both Windows and Macintosh operating systems. An optional rechargeable battery pack is also available for $80.

ADD-ONS AND PERIPHERALS

Best Computer Monitor (Tie): NEC E1100 and Nokia MultiGraph 445xi

Both sell for around $2,000

Nokia and NEC make the best 21-inch monitors in the business. Of course you pay for quality, but if you spend long hours staring at a computer screen the benefits outweigh the price tag.

Both monitors feature invar shadow mask tubes like those seen in state-of-the-art televisions, a 19.8-inch viewable image size, and resolution up to 1,600x1,200.

Best Computer Accessory: Iomega Zip and Jaz Drives

$200 for the Zip unit (including one disk)/**$15** for additional disks; **$500** for the Jaz unit (including one disk)/**$100** for additional disks.

Quite simply the best computer accessories of the decade (so far) are Iomega's Zip and Jaz portable hard drives. These items simply add new life to any computer—especially those with bulging hard disks. In case you are unfamiliar, both the Zip and Jaz operate in a similar fashion to floppy disks—except they hold a lot more. While a standard floppy disk holds up to 1.44 MB of data, a Zip disk holds up to 100 MB. That's about 70 times that of a standard floppy. It's almost the same size as a floppy, only a bit thicker. The Jaz is even more powerful as each disk holds 1 GB of data—that's roughly equivalent to ten Zip disks.

Both the Jaz and Zip are available in an outboard device that rests near the computer or an inboard unit that fits in most computers' drive bays. Since the portable drive mechanisms are relatively small, come with their own travel case, and connect quickly and easily, they make a lot of sense as they travel well between the home and office computer.

These add-ons are the ideal method of expanding your hard drive's capacity, as files can easily be transferred onto them and programs can reside on and run directly from them. Or, if your children are sharing your computer, you can place all of their programs and games on one (or more) of these disks to keep them from loading yet another version of DOOM on your hard drive. But the one factor I like about both of them is that they include software that virtually automates backing up your computer's hard drive.

Best Internet/Satellite Receiver: Hughes DirectDuo

$900 (for hardware)

This is the world's first digital satellite system that not only brings more than 200 digital channels to a television set, but delivers high-speed Internet access to a computer.

This system will connect to a television in a similar fashion as a standard DSS (see chapter 1), but it also includes a 16-bit ISA adapter card that slides into any Windows computer. This will enable Internet access times of up to 400 kbps. This speed is more than 14 times faster than a standard 28.8 kbps modem and 3 times the speed of an ISDN line.

The 21-inch-wide outside-mounted dish is larger than today's 18-inch models and, instead of being round, is elliptical. However it is important to note that this system will only receive the Internet data, it will not be able to transmit requests back to the host. This means that a phone line connection will still be necessary. But, understanding that sending commands to a specific Web site is relatively quick, and the slow speeds are caused by heavy graphic information being transmitted over phone lines back to your computer, this system will be a noticeable improvement over current send-and-receive modems.

Best Computer Monitor Television: Princeton Arcadia Home Monitor

$800

Last year's big buzzword was "convergence." This word referred to the merging of computers and televisions. While some thought that a product called the WebTV would be the answer it really never caught on despite all the hype. Others thought that massive computer systems that included large television monitors would be the answer. The jury is still out on that one.

For those who are looking for a more affordable method of bringing the computer into the living room I present the Arcadia monitor. Simply stated, this is a 27- or 31-inch television without the tuner. It allows for the connection of a computer as well as up to four different video sources such as a VCR, DVD, or satellite receiver. This way you can use its PIP mode to surf the Net while you watch the *Today* show. Or use the same set to play the latest CD-ROM game that you use to watch the *Today* show. (Okay, I'm pushing the *Today* show.) A more practical scenario is watching Greg Maddux pitching a game while viewing his lifetime stats on the Internet. You can even balance your checkbook while watching the *Love Boat* if you wish.

Best "Plug" for the PC: American Power Conversion Back-UPS Office

$180

Although you may never notice it, your computer can experience more than 100 power disturbances each month. Whether the problem is a power surge (too much electricity pumped into the computer) or a power outage, the effects of a power disturbance can seriously damage any computer.

The most common method of protecting against a power surge is a power strip, also known as a surge protector. However, considering that most of us use these strips for a variety of peripherals, they often offer less than adequate protection for your computer.

American Power Conversion's Back-UPS Office promises ample protection against power disturbances. Although at first glance it looks like a standard power strip, the difference is the rechargeable battery backup system that is concealed inside its casing.

The battery protects three of the six outlets, providing up to 13 minutes of continued usage during a power surge or failure. So if the power goes out while you are working, you'll have ample time to save your work and properly shut down the equipment.

The three protected outlets are designed for volatile hardware units (computer, monitor, modem, or printer). The other three can be used for other equipment, such as computer speakers.

Best Radio Device for the PC: Minolta PCFM

$50

It is nearly impossible to find a computer that does not include stereo speakers. But try to find one that includes an FM stereo radio—very few do. If you think about it, the inclusion of a radio with a computer makes sense—it would allow you to utilize the computer's enhanced audio system to listen to your favorite station while working on a program.

That's the concept behind Minolta's PCFM. This is a tiny device that attaches to your computer's serial port and connects to its sound card to add a full-function (87.5 to 108 MHz) FM stereo radio.

It features software that creates an on-screen control panel that offers a ten-station preset memory that enables you to store stations either by frequency number or by station call letters. Also included are step-and-scan tuning and volume controls.

Like a clock radio, it allows for sleep and wake-up timing but the computer has to be left on for these functions to operate properly. It also allows for up to five minutes of off-the-air recording directly onto the computer's hard drive.

PCFM is compatible with any Windows operating system, includes a dipole antenna, requires no external power, and delivers exactly what it promises.

Best Multimedia Speakers: Advent AV570

$400

For the best boom (literally) for the buck in audio for your computer, check out this two-speaker package from Advent.

Each speaker has a wedge-shaped design that allows it to fit nicely on your desktop, plus a built-in 35-watt amplifier with bass and treble controls. The speakers are made of aluminum alloy cabinetry and available in black or a "putty" computer-gray. Each speaker measures 10½x6½x7⅜ in.

Best New Use of Internet: Audio Highway Listen Up

$300

The Internet has proven to the world that it is an affordable and efficient method of putting vast quantities of information in the hands of consumers. Now there's a product, Audio Highway's palm-sized Listen Up, that allows you to download audio information (i.e., news, sports, languages, stocks) off the Net from your PC to a tiny handheld device and listen to it just about anywhere, whether it's your morning commute, red-eye flight, or car pool.

Here's how it works: To access information, just use any Internet browser to access the Audio Highway at http://www.audiohwy.com and launch the Audio Wizard software. Audio Highway has entered into contracts with more than 20 content providers, including the Associated

Press, Audio Scholar, Berlitz, MCA, and *Newsweek*, that will provide information to be downloaded.

You can either download up to an hour's worth of audio programming directly into the Listen Up or even longer lengths onto your computer's hard drive. It takes about 47 minutes to transfer an hour's worth of programming with a 28.8 kbps modem.

For those who spend time on airplanes or commuting to and from work on a train or other mode of transportation, using a notebook computer to hold the audio makes a lot of sense. This way, you can upload the information from your computer to the Listen Up at home, listen to the first hour, and then use the docking port to transfer the additional information from the computer to the handheld unit. Allow me to note that since this method of transfer uses the computer's parallel port, it takes only a few minutes to send the information from the computer to the handheld unit.

If you choose to download the information with the commercials (six minutes of commercials per hour) the programming is free. However, if you choose to bypass the ads, the cost is about $2 per hour.

Its software allows you to set up the unit to automatically download specific programs unattended, or have it search for specific news by category or company name.

Although it includes the ear-bud earphone, standard Walkman-style headphones can be used, or the programming can be played back on its incorporated speaker. Or, if you are in a car, you can use the cassette adapter and listen to it through your car's stereo system.

Also available is a car stereo transmitter that can send the signal up to 20 feet and be received on a predesignated frequency on any FM radio.

The Listen Up can also function as a handheld digital dictation device with three folders for categorization of messages.

SOFTWARE

**Best SOHO Software:
Microsoft Office 97
(Small Business Edition)**

$450

When the reviews first started rolling in for Microsoft's Office 97, they were less than flattering. But I honestly feel that reviewers who did not understand its capabilities performed the initial reviews of Microsoft's Office 97 too quickly. That's why I delayed my review until I could have my entire office setup—14 computers—loaded with this program.

If you look at this program as an upgraded word processor, spreadsheet, and database program, you might be disappointed. That's because although the software works well on a single computer, it truly stands out when used as a master program for multiple computers. It has the best spelling/grammar checker on the market today. It is a breeze to slip from one application to another and copy and paste data to and from each program. Its Intranet e-mail is the best in the business and truly puts Lotus Notes to shame. Although this program has some minor flaws such as not being able to open two word processing documents simultaneously, at press time Microsoft was hard at work repairing these flaws. I think the only problem with this program is the same with other Microsoft products—it was rushed to market. But they usually volunteer to fix any flaws in the program in a timely manner.

There are two versions of Office 97—standard and professional. The standard program includes MS Word, a word processing program with the best intuitive grammar and spell checker on the market; MS Excel, a spreadsheet program for managing your finances; MS Publisher, for creating professional brochures and newsletters; Automap Streets Plus, for finding where you are going; and MS Outlook, a calendar/time manager that consolidates all your activities (i.e., e-mail, phone messages, schedule), and also has networking features.

For larger offices Microsoft's Office 97 Professional Edition excludes the Automap program but adds advanced networking capabilities and a database manager called MS Access.

Best Organization Software: Day-Timer Organizer 2.1

$60

The new Day-Timer Organizer 2.1 offers the same take-it-with-you convenience of your paper-based organizer, but with the power of your computer. And when you've finally got everything organized onto your software, you can print your schedule and address book onto Day-Timer pages that will fit into your paper organizer. It features a

daily, weekly, and monthly planner that allows recurring events to be scheduled with a single entry. It also provides search and sort features and a built-in alarm, complete with a snooze option. Additionally, you can keep up to 35 pages of notes and 6 phone numbers for each of your contacts. The Day-Timer Organizer 2.1 software is compatible with both Mac and Windows operating systems.

Best Small Office Internet Solution: HotOffice

$25/mo. (per person)

If you need to get your business on the Internet and your employees on an e-mail system, but don't want to buy a $10,000 server and hire a $75,000-a-year tech guy to keep it up, check out HotOffice.

HotOffice is a private online service for your business. It is completely maintained and developed by the HotOffice staff according to your specifications for just $25 per month per person.

Once you subscribe, the HotOffice staff sets your business up with its own Web site, complete with e-mail addresses for you and your staff, gives your company a virtual file room so you can access any information you need while traveling, and offers chat rooms for online conferences and links to other business-related sites.

As a bonus, HotOffice provides a huge database of business and tax forms that you can download for billing, payroll, and other documentation.

Best Finance Software: Quicken

$60

If you are among the many who purchased a new computer to help organize your finances, the best program to help you achieve this goal is Quicken. In fact, and you will very seldom hear me say something like this, if you could buy only one productivity program for your computer, this is the one.

The true benchmark of a good program is its ability to simplify complicated tasks, and Quicken gets top marks in this department. The program displays an on-screen, fill-in-the-blank check form. All you have to do is assign each check a category, such as rent, mortgage, clothes, automotive, etc., and the program automatically files expenditures under the proper heading.

At any time, a couple of clicks of the mouse button instruct the program to generate a report that is so detailed it could lower your accountant's fees. Other features include simplified checkbook balancing, tax scheduling, budgeting, graphing, and electronic banking. Of course, you can order computer checks, print them out on your printer, and never handwrite one again. Available for Macintosh and Windows.

Best Children's Software: Living Books

$35

With a plethora of CD-ROMs on the market for young children, it's difficult to choose just the right one for your child. Our experience reviewing hundreds, if not thousands, of software titles is that less than 20 percent are worth the money. Why? Most of the titles are designed by gear heads, not parents. Sure, some of the graphics are outstanding and story lines okay, but it takes a special talent to capture the attention, entertain, and educate three- to seven-year-olds.

Living Books is an exception to the rule. Its titles include Dr. Seuss's *ABC's* and *Green Eggs and Ham, Stellaluna,* and *Sheila Rhea the Brave.* Each title is parent friendly—meaning you can choose to have the story read to your child. This allows you to get up and shake out the leg cramps from junior sitting in your lap and not worry about clicking the mouse to advance the page. As your child progresses, you can choose other options that allow him or her to interact with the story lines. Best of all the Living Books titles teach without appearing to. They truly make learning fun for the younger set.

Best Software/Hardware Music Tutor: Piano Discovery

$99

Piano Discovery is an on-screen music tutor that comes with a 49-key electronic keyboard (that connects to the computer's parallel port) and software for one year of piano lessons.

Designed for ages six to adult, it features on-screen graphics, voice prompts, and interactive games to make learning how to read and play music more fun than work. Once you have mastered a song, you can take it to its jam stage and play it along with a full orchestra. It includes positive reinforcement and 50 songs from Bach to rock. Additional lesson packs cost $80 each.

Best Travel Software: TravRoute Road Trips: Door-to-Door (1997 edition)

$50

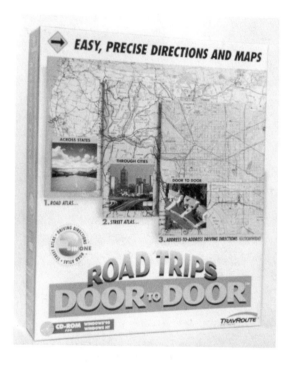

Using your computer to assist in planning a summer car trip is a concept that has grown tremendously over the past few years. Not only is it a productive way to plan a trip, it is an exercise the entire family can partake in. Even better, if your children help plan the routes, and print out maps of the trip, instead of asking "are we there yet?" they can see how long it will take to get to their destination. This season's hot traveling title is Road Trips: Door-to-Door. This program not only allows you to enter your origination and destination cities, but also enables you to enter specific addresses so you can literally route your trip from your home to the front door of your destination.

It features a split screen that shows the itinerary, complete with mileage and travel time, and a detailed map that shows your route along the way. It also allows up to 15 stops and alternative scenic routes, as well as variables for different types of roads and desirable cruising speeds.

For the more serious traveler, or if you just really want to impress your friends, there's a new version of Door-to-Door called Co-Pilot ($350) that comes with a global positioning system (GPS) satellite navigation device that connects to your PC or laptop. Together with the software, this allows you to track a vehicle's real time location via satellite on the Door-to-Door map. This will truly keep the children occupied.

Best Cooking Software: Mangia

$35

With more than 800 recipes and room to include your own favorite concoctions, Mangia is the best virtual cookbook on the market.

This electronic cookbook makes meal-planning, recipe selection, and even shopping easier than ever. It features an intuitive search engine that can locate recipes by ingredients, cooking time, difficulty, course, or even nationality. It allows you to print recipe cards, pages, and booklets using its bundled fonts and professionally designed formats—you can even create your own cookbook.

Mangia also has scaling capabilities, which allow you to enter the number of portions needed and automatically provide you with the adjusted ingredients. There's also a nutritional analysis meter with low-fat substitutions. Shopping lists are simplified too, as the program automatically omits ingredients you already have in your pantry and organizes ingredients by the section of the store where they are found, allowing you to print a custom shopping list. Available for Mac and Windows.

Best Movie Software: Microsoft Cinemania

$35

If you are a movie buff, the best and most informative silver screen software on the market is Microsoft's Cinemania.

This Windows-only (hey, it's published by Microsoft) CD-ROM features comments and critiques from Leonard Maltin, Pauline Kael, and Roger Ebert and comes packed with information on more than 20,000 titles, including 30 full motion-video clips, and 4,500 profiles of directors, writers, and other movie professionals. It even has a Cinemania suggest function that helps you select a movie when you can't decide what to see. To keep it up-to-date, purchasers can, for one year, go to the Cinemania Internet site for free updates. After the first year, you have to buy a new copy. But hey, it's only $35.

Best Bizarre Title: You Don't Know Jack

$35

Game show addicts can now turn off the TV and turn on the computer for a top-notch quiz show program.

This adult-oriented interactive game show has the look and feel of a real on-the-air experience and features more than 1,200 off-the-wall multiple choice trivia questions that are ideal for parties or for joking it up by yourself. What really gives this program high marks is its fast-paced action and irreverent and insincere game show host who not only deals out the questions but barrages the player with hilarious and sometimes sassy abuse. Allow me to reiterate, though, that this game is for adults, not children.

Also available are a sports and movie trivia pack.

Best Imaging Software: Adobe Photo Deluxe

$90

With digital cameras, scanners, and photo-quality printers all the rage, to fully take advantage of home photo manipulation, a good image-processing program is required. The only problem with this is that most of the image-processing programs on the market require a degree from MIT to operate. But Photo Deluxe is a scaled-down, easier-to-use version of Adobe's award-winning PhotoShop. Designed for the rookie, it makes touching-up photos and graphic designing a piece of cake. It features more than 25 easy-to-use functions for scanned photos, ranging from personalized calendars to special effects to on-screen slide shows. Available for Macintosh and Windows.

Best Software to Split With: DIVORCE from E-Z Legal

$30

These days, you can do just about anything with a personal computer. You can write a letter and e-mail it around the world, gather real time news and stock quotes from the Internet, even design your dream home. Now there is one that lets you break it up.

Yes, DIVORCE from E-Z Legal is the first do-it-yourself divorce kit that is valid in all 50 states. It features an easy-to-use, fill-in-the-blank format that enables couples with no minor children and no major real estate to follow a step-by-step process to prepare their own basic divorce documents, thus bypassing expensive legal fees. It even advises on how to consult with the local court system for filing procedures. On-screen help is also included.

In more complex divorce situations, DIVORCE prepares couples for the legal issues that are sure to surface during lengthy procedures. The program links with its Web site (http://e-zlegal.com), allowing couples to review updated local legal statutes and divorce laws. E-Z Legal advises, however, that since statutes may vary, users contact their local courts for specific filing instructions.

DIVORCE is packaged with both CD-ROM and floppy disks and supports all Windows formats. To reduce my own legal liability, allow me to add that in reviewing this program, I am not a lawyer, nor do I play one on TV.

PERSONAL ORGANIZERS

There are two types of people in this world: those who use personal organizers and those who don't.

You know the ones who do—they are prompt for appointments, can always find a phone or fax number, and never forget anniversaries. Those who don't are the ones that send belated birthday cards and show up two days late for Uncle Bernie's surprise party.

In case you're not familiar with them, pocket (or electronic) organizers are handheld calculator look-alikes that allow you to store and recall names, addresses, and phone numbers as well as keep track of your appointments. The latest batch of pocket organizers even allows for the transmission of faxes and connection to an e-mail service.

When shopping for an organizer, the first decision you have to make is how much memory you will need. This decision will ultimately be based on the quantity of information you are planning to store. Today's models include memories ranging from 8 KB to 8 MB. A system with 64 KB of memory can hold up to 64,000 characters; each character is equal to one press on the keyboard. However, each organizer reserves a certain amount of memory for various built-in functions such as the clock and calculator as well as the operating system, so 64 KB would translate into about 45 KB of usable memory.

So, how much memory do you need? A typical address book listing is comprised of about 75 characters, so you would be able to store around 600 entries in a typical 64 KB unit. Some units are upgradable and allow for the insertion of additional memory modules. Most offer cables that allow them to connect to a computer for backup.

Having tested just about every model on the market, I can say with good authority that there is no such thing as the perfect pocket organizer. The reason I say this is that, despite all the bells and whistles included on the latest units—such as e-mail, faxing, spreadsheets, and word processing—when it comes down to it a good name database and agenda are really the only practical uses of these tiny wonders. That's because unless you're Tom Thumb, typing on tiny keyboards is about as rewarding as trying to thread a needle, not to mention what reading e-mail, faxes, and word processing documents on a miniscule 2-inch screen can do to your eyes.

So why, you may ask, can't I live without these miracles of modern technology? Because I believe there is no better way to keep your appointments and contacts. Not just current appointments, but past ones too, as the latest models allow you to review and archive all your activities. Plus they are fast. Consider how long it takes to start your laptop computer and find a name or appointment; and despite its desktop convenience, a paper-based organizer is equally as cumbersome when away from the office. So for their convenience, efficiency, and best of all size, an electronic pocket organizer truly is your ticket to increased productivity.

Best Pocket Organizer:
U.S. Robotics Palm Pilot
(Runners-Up: Sharp Mobile Organizer
SE-500 and Psion Series 5)

$300 (Palm Pilot, Sharp);
$600 (Psion)

You could almost hear the sounds of people tossing their existing bulky organizers out the windows when U.S. Robotics introduced the Palm Pilot. Sized about the same as a deck of cards—only thinner—this pen-based organizer includes 1 MB of memory and bypasses the keyboard in favor of an easy-to-learn and -use Graffiti handwriting recognition system; an on-screen keyboard may be selected with a simple penstroke.

What I like best about this device is that it eliminates the fluff and features you will probably never use and concentrates on the core functions—appointment and telephone book—that in my opinion make the personal organizer a must-have.

For further proof that the Palm Pilot is the hottest product around, perennial organizer sales leader Sharp has introduced a Pilot-like device called the Mobile Organizer. Sized just a bit larger than the Palm Pilot, it features a built-in 14.4 kpbs modem and a unique flip-top plastic cover, making it the ideal second choice—that is, if the store is sold out of Pilots.

The best features-laden organizer on the market is Psion's Series 5. With up to 8 MB of memory, this unit includes not only a pen for navigation (not handwriting) but the best keyboard and screen size around. Its 32-bit processor makes it the fastest on the market, and its agenda and database are, bar none, the best in the business. I will, however, take issue with Psion's synchronization software, which, unless you went to MIT, is difficult at best and performs at a level far below the aforementioned models.

Best New Organizer Category to Watch: Windows CE

$500+

If you own a computer equipped with Windows 95, you may want to check out the latest development in the organizer category, something called HPC (for "handheld PC"). HPCs feature Windows CE, a specially developed operating system from Microsoft. Although nobody knows for sure what *CE* stands for, I think it means "compact edition" or "consumer electronics." Data, files, and other information may be transferred simply and quickly from a Windows 95–based computer to the HPC with either a docking station and cable connected to the PC or wirelessly, via infrared beams—if your PC has an infrared transmitter. Although transmission via cable is faster, infrared transfer is easier. Windows CE comes equipped with "pocket" versions of Microsoft Excel, Word, Microsoft Internet Explorer, and Inbox (for e-mail)—all of which make exchanging files with desktop counterparts a simple process. It also has a built-in scheduler, address book, and spreadsheet.

I've found the CE units, like other first-generation products, to be a little underwhelming at best. Although these models can be difficult to read and are slower than others currently on the market, I am hoping that the second generation (due this year) will cure these ills. In fact, I've heard from Microsoft that the CE version 2 will offer a color 256 k screen, a zoom function that will make its small fonts easier to read, an improved interface, and better interaction with the desktop computer. Some models will even allow for connection to an auxiliary monitor and grant remote synchronization. In the meantime, products like the Cassiopeia (pictured above), the Philips Velo (fastest), and the Hewlett Packard 300LX Palmtop (best keyboard and screen) are my picks in this growing category of HPCs.

CHAPTER 5

Sporting Goods

The sporting goods industry in many ways is like the high-tech industry. While prices may not become lower each and every year, the products continue to advance consistently. Back in my early teens, I just didn't think bicycles could get any better than my banana seat model with ape-hanger handlebars. Today, they have automatic transmissions. In the skiing world, it seemed for a while that the only thing new about skis were the colors and composite materials hidden beneath the exterior. Today, the hottest thing going is parabolic skis that allow intermediate skiers to ski with more control and grace than ever before.

So, in the words of some Madison Avenue whiz kid, let's Just Do It.

BICYCLES

Sometimes life is just too complicated. Take bicycles, for example. What used to be a pretty simple product category has grown so complex you need a degree in astrophysics just to determine which bike is right for you. It seems that just finding the right gear to pedal in can be a nightmare. But let's face it, except for those planning to ascend Mount McKinley or ride the Tour de France, most of us just need a bike that is comfortable and easy to operate.

Best Cruising Bike: CSA AutoBike

$360

What separates this bike from the rest is that it is the only one with an automatic transmission—meaning you don't have to worry about changing gears; it automatically changes gears to match your cycling speed. This means that whether you're climbing a hill or just cruising along, no cumbersome gear-shifting is required.

Here's how it works: Counterweights are positioned on the rear spokes of the bike. As you speed up, centrifugal force causes the weights to move upward along the spokes, automatically shifting the bike to a higher gear. As you slow down, the weights automatically move toward the center of the wheel hub, causing the shift to a lower, easier gear.

The manufacturer claims that this 6-speed bike has the same gear range as a 21-speed bike, but without the unnecessary gears. The bike comes with 26-inch all-terrain tires; a comfortable extra-wide spring-cushion seat; a lightweight 34-pound steel frame; hand brakes; a kick-stand; and sure-grip foot pedals—all combined with the classic styling of the cruiser bicycles of yesteryear.

Available in two styles for both men and women: The Classic ($360) is a replica of the classic beach-cruiser bicycle, and the Cruiser Elite ($400) is a complete 1950s retro-cruiser with whitewall tires and chrome fenders.

Best Retro Bike: Schwinn Cruiser Deluxe

$480

Take a ride down memory lane with this retro single-speed cruising bike. Okay, it doesn't have a banana seat, but it does have whitewall tires, a spring seat, and a replica of the classic Schwinn cantilever frame (built to

spec from the original 1955 blueprints). But that's not all, this bike also includes the original chrome black phantom springer fork on the front that made this bike the envy of every kid on the block.

It is available in cream/green or dark blue/blue. If you're really feeling nostalgic, Schwinn is also offering an original black phantom replica with all the bells and whistles for $3,000. If you think this bike is priced out of everyone's reach, think again. There must be a lot of baby boomers wanting to relive their youth; a local bike shop told me that he had deposits on this bike before they ever hit the store. I guess this is the Harley-Davidson of bicycles.

Best Bike Concept: Zap ElectriCruizer

$849

This is a bike with a twist—it has a battery-powered motor that gets you around town or around the block.

Connected underneath the bike's seat is a 22-pound battery power system that is attached to its rear wheel. To engage, all you do is flip a switch and the Zap motor will deliver you at speeds up to 20 miles per hour. You can deactivate the motor anytime you wish and pedal. Battery life is 20 miles with a recharge time of 2 to 3 hours. Its steel frame is equipped with a 6-speed grip throttle and front and rear cantilever brakes. Wide whitewall tires and a springy seat help smooth the bumpiest roads. The curved handlebars make for a comfortable upright riding position as well. Plus, with the Zap power system, you can make molehills out of the mountains you used to have to climb! A Zap motor system that fits most bicycles is also available for $450.

SKATES

Whoever thought that in-line skates would catch on? Well, they have. In fact, they are so popular that it's difficult, if not impossible, to go to a public park and not see hordes of in-line skaters. Because of a smoother ride and good protective gear, these things have won the hearts (and wallets) of just about every age bracket. But, it is important to note that learning to use in-line skates can take a while, so make sure you are wearing the right protective gear. In most cases this consists of a good helmet and wrist, knee, and elbow pads. But once you've caught the hang of it, in-line skating is a blast. Not only is it a good workout, it is fun. If ice cream could make you lose weight, it would be flavored "in-line."

Best In-Line Skates: K-2 Impulse
$300

One major drawback to an in-line skate has been its comfort factor. That's because a big hard-shell plastic boot just doesn't feel good. Solving this dilemma are the K-2 in-line skates with a unique soft boot design.

More like hiking boots than in-line skates, these wheeled wonders are not only comfortable but provide exceptional lateral support too. Each skate is made of leather and a breathable mesh with cuffs for ankle support. But that's not all. K-2's new skates feature a smartfit gel pad that conforms to your foot and ankle structure. As the foot heats during skating, the gel firms, holding the foot and ankle in place, creating support. When you remove your foot, the gel softens, waiting for your next adventure.

Best In-Line Skates for Kids: Rollerblade XtenBlade

$100

If buying shoes for the kids isn't hard enough, imagine what it's like buying skates—kids practically grow out of them on the way home from the store. This means that during their formative years, you will constantly be asked if they can have some money for yet another pair. To the rescue comes the Rollerblade XtenBlade.

Designed for kids, these innovative in-line skates actually grow with your child's feet. That's because with a quick adjustment you can make the skate size up to four sizes larger, beginning at size 12-2, then size 1-4, and finally size 3-6. That means one pair should last for years. Although this is a novel and practical approach for in-line skates, it is not a new idea. Remember the skate key? Now if they could only figure how to make the rest of your kids' stuff grow too.

SKIS

Best New Concept Ski: Elan Parabolic

$400

If you purchased a new pair of snow skis in the past two years and thought they would last for many seasons to come, I have bad news for you.

There's been a major breakthrough in ski design, and it might just make you want to rush out and buy a brand-new pair. Called the hourglass ski, this innovative new design makes it simpler than ever for beginning and intermediate skiers to chute down the slopes. Wide in the front and rear and thin in the middle (hence the name "hourglass"), these skis are easier to balance on than conventional skis, and their design helps accelerate the learning process by simplifying such maneuvers as carving and turning. (The model is fast becoming a staple in ski schools around the world.)

The skis feature a deep side-cut that matches the turn radius of the skier, allowing for more control and less skidding at any speed. The leading manufacturer of hourglass skis is Elan, maker of the SCX line. Elan is offering two models, and although they are similarly shaped, the beginner's model (the SCX Parabolic Cap) has more flexibility (and rigidity) where needed, while the intermediate-to-advanced model (the SCX Monoblock) offers more performance features.

Best Boots for Hourglass Skis: Dolomite CYB-X "Carve Series"

$350

Hourglass, or parabolic, skis have become so popular that there's now even a boot designed especially for them. Dolomite's CYB-X boots incorporate a profile lift sole that raises the skier's stance 15 mm. This dramatically increases the amount of leverage skiers can transmit to the edge of the ski, and translates into even easier, more confident turns for any skill-level skier.

Best New Ski Bindings: Salomon Spheric Binding

$210

All snow skiers have at least one "agony of defeat" wipeout story to tell.

Unfortunately many of these spills result in what has become the most common injury on the slopes today—a torn anterior cruciate ligament (ACL), more commonly called a busted knee. Studies show that about 85 percent of these injuries can be attributed to the ski binding (the bracket that clamps the boot to the ski) not releasing. That's because ski bindings do not release in a forward fall. Until now.

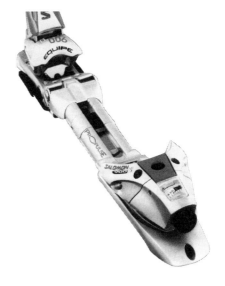

The best new ski binding on the market is Salomon's new Spheric Binding—the world's first model that releases in the event of a forward-rolling fall. In fact, these bindings are such an improvement over traditional bindings that Salomon is dubbing them "air bags for skis."

Unlike the traditional binding, which has a two-axis system that releases the boot from the ski when the skier twists and falls toward the left or right, the Spheric binding adds a third axis that recognizes a forward fall and releases the boot when forward pressure is detected.

For a more comfortable ride the bindings also include a mini shock absorber under the heel that cushions the boot from the ski and assists in steering and mobility.

Best High-Tech Ski: K-2's Merlin 5

$750

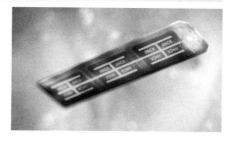

Dubbed the world's first "ski with a brain," this ski incorporates electronic circuitry that converts low-frequency vibrations into electrical energy. This energy is then transferred to a front-mounted module that channels the power to the edges of the ski, which in turn provides for a smoother ride. Really! Allow me to note that, being intermediate skiers, neither Kelley nor I tested these high-performance skis. However, on our *Today* piece at Sunday River, Maine, the ski instructors went bonkers over these skis.

The Merlin 5 also features a small green LED light that illuminates to show the skier that it is working. It is currently available and retails for $750 per pair. Now, if only they made these in a parabolic style . . .

CAMPING

Best Lantern: Coleman NorthStar Propane Lantern

$50

Forget messy fuels and batteries, Coleman's new propane-powered lantern gives you light when you need it.

Featuring a matchless one-push electronic ignition and 20 percent more luminance than current lanterns, this unit runs off a 1-pound propane canister that lasts for days at full charge. Other features include a sturdy globe guard cage and an easy-to-replace mantle with no strings to tie (unlike other units).

Best Flashlight: Panasonic Taskmaster

$13

Because you often need two hands when camping, this flashlight from Panasonic is attached to a wearable headband.

Powered by 4 AA batteries, this headband light is great for reading or just trying to locate the restroom in a dark campground. To use, just strap it around your head and twist the outer shell, and voilà! instant headlight. And the best thing of all is that it sells for only $13.

Best Kid Carrier Backpack: Tough Traveler Child Carrier

$99

A backpack with a detachable diaper bag and changing pad? You got it. The Tough Traveler Child Carrier (tried and tested by Mr. Kelley) is the best way to transport baby from point A to point B.

Great for hiking in the mountains or just around town, the Tough Traveler features sturdy aluminum support and a waistband attachment for the best comfort fit in kid carrier backpacks. It supports children up to 55 pounds and has a number of unique accessories like a rain hood and a mosquito net for baby's first subterranean expedition. Also check out Tough Traveler's Baby Bear, a custom sleeping bag for two- to three-year-olds.

Best Binoculars: Minolta UCII

$182

Whether you're camping, at the ball game, or at the opera, Minolta's tiny UC (ultra compact) binoculars bring you closer to the action.

Billed as the world's smallest and lightest roof-prism binoculars, this 3.4x1⅘₂₅x⅘ in. model from Minolta fits in a shirt pocket and weighs only 5.11 ounces.

Delivering 6X magnification, the UCII can even focus on an object as close as 3⅓ feet—the shortest focus distance in the business.

Best Hiking Boots: AD One Xplora

$75

Equally at home in the mountains or on city streets, these Italian leather hiking shoes are not only stylish but can handle the elements too.

The Xplora boot features a 100 percent waterproof lining, a breathable oiled leather exterior, and a unique interior lining that wicks away moisture for maximum comfort. Best of all they look great.

Best Product for Indiana Jones: Magellan System GPS 2000

$200

When you stop and think about it, global positioning systems are absolutely amazing devices. These are handheld, calculator-style instruments that read signals from numerous satellites and can tell you in an instant exactly where you are. More important, they can tell you how to get back. Fishermen

(or fisherwomen) love them as well, as they can mark their favorite fishing spots and be guided back there time after time.

Great for hiking or boating, the Magellan is easy to use too. Just mark your position (i.e., campground) by pressing a button. Hike as long as you want and periodically mark your position. When you want to go back, press "go to marked" button, and the unit then tells you how far away your original spot is, how long it takes to get back, and displays on its LCD screen a map of how to get there. Powered by 4 AAA batteries, it measures 6⅜x2⅛x⅓ in.

CHAPTER 6

Big Toys for Aging Boomers

Probably the best part of my job is being able to cover topics that are not only newsworthy but also those that I consider hobbies.

For me, motorcycles, sports cars, and boats fit into this category. (Am I going through a midlife crisis or what?) So sit back and enjoy the ride as we give you our favorite picks for the year.

MOTORCYCLES

Although driving a sexy sports car or tooling around the lake on a personal watercraft is fun, cruising along the backroads of Tennessee on a motorcycle is truly relaxing. With my hectic travel schedule, motorcycling is the one recreation that I still hold sacred. These two-wheeled machines are an easy method of taking quick mini-vacations. No, not a week on the road, but a way to take an hour or so and turn it into a truly refreshing experience.

Part of my pleasure is derived from where I live. If I lived in New York City, a ride around the block would probably cause me more frustration than relaxation. Living in Nashville, though, is just the opposite. Just ten minutes from my home is what I consider the finest motorcycling venue in the world—the Natchez Trace Parkway. This smoothly paved historic route is loaded with twists and turns that deliver a great riding experience without the need to break the speed limit.

At a recent charity motorcycle ride called the Trace Tour—benefiting the Rochelle Center of Nashville, I cruised along with other bike lovers such as *Cycle World*'s editor Larry Little, *Playboy*'s Jim Peterson, music legend Lyle Lovett, NBC *Today* show producer Roland Woerner, photographer/writer Slick Lawson, and motorcycle aficionados Peter Bollenbach and Jim Lattimore.

These guys, like myself, lead busy lives. Although our social lives seldom cross, what we do have in common is a love for motorcycles. It is our way of escaping the hustle and bustle of our everyday lives.

When at a rest stop halfway through the trip, the grins on these guys' faces were definitely ear-to-ear. That's because the Natchez Trace Parkway is like no other road in the country. It is smooth and curvy, and because it is surrounded by the best nature has to offer, with no distracting billboards or road-hogging 18-wheelers, it provides for one of the most relaxing afternoon adventures anyone could ever ask for.

But there is something mysterious about motorcycles—they are the great equalizers. When you ride with a group of folks and stop and have lunch, you quickly realize that you don't care where they live, how much they make, or what kind of car they drive. The mealtime conversation runs the gamut of bikes—how to customize them, where to ride them, and how to make them sound better.

This brings up an important point: Not all bikes are created equal. While visiting the home of one of my riding buddies, Jim Lattimore, and entering his garage, my eyes feasted on nine—count 'em, nine—motorcycles. Of course, I had to ask him why he needed nine bikes. And Jim made a good point. He told me that there was no one perfect motorcycle. Where and what type of riding he wants to do dictates which bike he fires up.

Jim is absolutely correct. Although a sport bike may be ideal for the constant shifts in direction needed to navigate roads like the Trace, it would be uncomfortable on a long highway trip. In the reverse, a big cruiser or a highway-touring model can be hard to maneuver on constant tight turns.

The bottom line is that it would be great if we all could afford nine bikes—but we can't. So, before shopping for the right one for you, instead of selecting the prettiest one on the showroom floor, it would be wise to first decide which type of riding you will be doing the most.

However, before you reach into your wallet, there is one important step that any rider should proceed with—no matter what his or her riding skill—a training course.

The Motorcycle Safety Foundation is a national nonprofit organization that promotes the safety of motorcyclists with programs in rider training nationwide. Since its inception in 1973, the foundation has trained over one million students to ride safely. The foundation has more than 4,000 certified instructors that conduct weekend-long riding seminars at more than 800 sites in all 50 states.

Its entry-level course is a 15-hour classroom and riding program for new riders that provides motorcycle and protective gear for students' use. There's also a 7-hour course for experienced riders to fine-tune their skills. Before you buy a bike, or even if you own one, I highly recommend these classes. To find out more, call (800) 833-3995.

Best Entry-Level Motorcycle: Suzuki Savage LS650PV

$4,500

The smartest way to get into motorcycling is to start small and trade up. Smaller bikes are easier to handle, are more forgiving, and cost thousands of dollars less than their beefed-up counterparts. Even if you logged thousands of miles as a teenager and have decided to reenter the world of motorcycling, instead of starting with a $15,000 Harley-Davidson, you will be well advised to begin with a smaller, albeit wimpier, entry-level bike. This is my way of cautioning you not to have more dollars than sense. When the need arises, these small- to medium-sized models are relatively easy to resell. That's because when the weather turns nice there is always someone who decides that this is the year to either learn—or relearn—how to ride. Too many times a midlife crisis interferes with rational behavior and people end up with a gorgeous Harley that they never get to enjoy as they are too nervous trying to remember which gear is which. These models end up resting on display in the garage, and are seldom, if ever, placed on the road.

As I've mentioned, my best advice for new riders is to begin by taking a sanctioned riding class. After you've earned your license, then start with a bike that is easy to maneuver. This is the same advice I am giving John Kelley—as he has completed the riding class and is now shopping for a bike. After much deliberation, our pick for the best entry-level bike is the Suzuki Savage LS650PV.

Despite its intimidating name, and Harley look-alike styling, this cruising-class bike is easy to ride. It includes a 4-stroke 650cc engine, a comfortable seat, and a low 27.6-inch seat height. The low seat height is important for beginners as it allows you to easily keep your feet firmly on the ground when at a standstill. Other features include front disk brakes, rear drum brakes, and a 5-speed transmission. Best of all, at $4,500 you can learn the ropes without breaking the bank. If you decide you want a larger bike (and you will), you can trade it in the following season for a garaged-kept bike purchased by someone who did not have sense to read this book and heed my advice!

Best Highway Touring Motorcycle: Honda Gold Wing SE

$17,000

You've seen them on the highway—they look like two-wheeled Winnebagos that have a place for just about everything except the kitchen sink. They are large, cumbersome, and can be difficult to maneuver on tight turns. But, on the open road, there is no better, more comfortable ride than Honda's tried-and-tested Gold Wing SE.

The Gold Wing is truly the king of the open road as it is loaded with creature comforts such as the most ergonomic seating in the business, adjustable passenger footrests, an air-flow system for hot or cool air, and a built-in AM/FM stereo along with a CB radio. This model even includes a voice-activated intercom that allows the driver and passenger to communicate without having to scream at each other. But my favorite feature is its reverse gear. Anyone who has tried to backpedal a bike this large into or out of a parking space has learned that in some situations, this maneuver can be difficult if not impossible. The press of a lever allows this 815-pound behemoth to back out at a snail's pace on almost any grade of street. Of course the Wing is known for its storage, and there are enough compartments on this machine to pack for a month on the road.

The bottom line is that the Gold Wing SE earned this award for being the most comfortable ride on two wheels. This is the Rolls-Royce of touring motorcycles, a top-notch machine that makes mincemeat out of long trips. In fact, you can ride 1,000 miles on this bike without feeling like you were washed, rinsed, and put through the spin cycle.

Concealed beneath its fiberglass exterior is a powerful 1520cc liquid-cooled 6-cylinder engine—that's bigger than the economy engine found in Honda's Civic, and despite its size, its seat is only 29.1 inches from the ground—making it something that even my 5-foot, 6-inch frame can handle.

Best Cruising Motorcycle (Tie): Yamaha Royal Star Tour Deluxe and Harley-Davidson Road King

$15,000 (Yamaha); **$14,500** (Harley)

Although the important motorcycle manufacturers of the world have attempted to steal a piece of the pie away from Harley-Davidson, they have all failed. One reason is that although many imports are starting to look like Harleys, they don't even come close to sounding like one. What does a Harley sound like? Like this: P O T A T O, P O T A T O, P O T A T O.

However, there is a diamond in the rough of import cruisers and it is Yamaha's Royal Star Tour Deluxe. Introduced in 1996, this model delivers a solid ride and confuses passersby into thinking it's a Harley. In fact, when I was setting up a recent *Today* show segment highlighting the hottest new motorcycles, I saw a trailer pull up to our studio with what I instantly thought was a Harley-Davidson Road King. Since I did not request that particular bike for the story, I turned to the Harley representative and asked her what that bike was doing here. At that moment Bob Star, the Yamaha representative, turned to me and said, "That's not a Road King, it's Yamaha's new Royal Star Tour Deluxe." Boy, was my face red—but not as much as the Harley representative's! One reason Yamaha has succeeded while others have failed is that they designed a bike that American riders can truly sink their teeth into and can accessorize to take on a personality all its own. Although some Harley riders may sneer at this model—being an import and all—after putting several thousand miles on a Royal Star I have to admit it is an excellent motorcycle. Although it does not sound like a Harley, a pair of Cobra replacement exhausts can give it a personality that makes you wonder why you wanted a Harley in the first place. Although it shares the fat tank styling, and much of the good looks, it has its own personality and delivers something that Harley-Davidsons usually do not—a smooth ride. Also, because of its 66.7-inch wheelbase, it is virtually resistant to the gusts of wind that follow the big trucks and is kept firmly on the ground.

The Royal Star features a big, fat comfortable seat and large saddlebags that deliver some of the best storage found on any cruiser. It comes stocked with a windshield—a necessity for highway driving—and features a 1294cc water-cooled 4-stroke engine. The bike weighs in at a respectable 672 pounds and has a seat height of 28.1 inches.

With more Americans turning fifty than ever before in history, the folks at Harley must be shimmying in their leathers. Because nothing satisfies a midlife crisis more than a big fat Hog strapped between your legs.

The best Harley for a midlife crisis is without a doubt the Road King. Guaranteed to restore your testosterone to teenage levels with just one twist of the throttle, this 1340cc machine delivers the right power and the sound to match. Although not my first choice for a cross-country journey, it can definitely accomplish the job. This model has a fatter feel than Harley's Softail models, which results in a strong but stable riding machine; when riding it, the only thought that comes to mind is there is nothing like a Harley. Because of better shock absorbers and rubber engine mounts, your world won't get rocked while cruising down the highway. In fact, it is more at home at 65 MPH than it is at 30 MPH.

Other features include a nostalgic giant headlight, detachable fiberglass saddlebags, and a removable acrylic windshield as well as Harley's trademark—chromed everything (almost). And if you want more chrome, don't worry. The dealer can make this thing so shiny that you'll need sunglasses just to view it under the lights. And this year the folks at Harley-Davidson have added a new feature: fuel injection. This provides for effortless starting in all weather conditions. The only negative is that it alters the sound of those pipes.

The Road King weighs in at 692 pounds and has a 28.2-inch seat height. Of course, Harleys are made to be modified, so expect to customize—it's the Harley way.

Best Sport Bike: Yamaha YZF600R

$7,300

The folks in the motorcycle industry really get ticked off when their sporty bikes are referred to as "crotch rockets." But that's the jargon that has come to describe these high-tech machines.

Designed to look fast, even when they are standing still, these swift accelerators are ridden in a near-prone position. This form grants the driver complete control of the machine and allows it to zip through curves like no other category of motorcycle in the world.

I'd originally thought these models were designed more for the twenty-something set than for those my age, but after spending some time on them I've begun changing my tune.

The YZF600R from Yamaha was designed from the ground up to be the most aerodynamic sport bike in its class. With a low-slung front café-style fairing and side deflectors, this bike earns its wings (almost literally) and allows the bike to cut through wind with almost no resistance. It is powered by a 600cc liquid-cooled 16-valve, 4-cylinder engine that delivers a top speed (140 MPH) that is faster than that of most small airplanes.

On the other side of the control issue, it includes an innovative 4-piston front and rear disk brake system with pressure balancers that deliver fast no-skid stops.

Allow me to note that although on paper a 600cc engine might seem tiny compared with the aforementioned cruisers, this bike can, at speeds of up to 140 MPH, truly leave the 1340cc models eating dust. That's because the engines are completely different. While other models deliver a more comfortable upright ride, this model is designed for speed and low-slung handling with high torque levels.

BEST NEW CARS FOR RECEDING HAIRLINES

Let's face it: Not all of us get our jollies on a motorcycle. The rest of us find the ultimate cure to the midlife crisis by cruising around in a spiffy sports car. I guess this thinking falls in the category of "The difference between a man and a boy is the size and the price of his toys."

The good news is that the automobile manufacturers of the world have finally delivered sports cars that are somewhat affordable. No longer do we have to spend upwards of $90,000 for a Mercedes convertible or sexy Porsche; we can get new sports cars for less than half that price. Although the monthly payments will rival a house mortgage, these models deliver the best bang-for-the-buck in history.

The bad news is they can be hard to get. This new generation of lower-priced sports cars is selling as fast as the manufacturers can make them—so you may have to plunk down a deposit just to get on the waiting list. The other bit of bad news is that they won't grow your hair back, but they will give you an excuse for buying a spiffy hat—and when you're behind the wheel, no one will laugh at you, but they most definitely will become jealous.

Until now it has been almost impossible to even think about buying new cars from the likes of Porsche, BMW, and Mercedes Benz without spending megabucks. That has changed. In an effort to appeal to younger (read: well-to-do but not necessarily super-rich) buyers, all four manufacturers recently introduced entirely new vehicles aimed squarely at that market. Porsche brought out the Boxster, the first all-new Porsche in nineteen years; Chevrolet introduced the C-5 Corvette, which is only the fifth "new from the ground up" Corvette since 1953; BMW showed its new Z3 roadster; and Mercedes Benz unveiled the revolutionary new SLK hard-top convertible. These four vehicles are all very well equipped and priced under $40,000.

Despite many similarities, after testing these vehicles (yes, it's a tough job, but somebody's got to do it) I noticed that each of these cars has its own distinctive personality. It is also interesting to observe the way manufacturers, all starting with a clean sheet of paper, approached the same target group.

Best New BMW: Z3 2.8

$35,900 (list)

The BMW Z3 is a real sports car in true BMW style. It is based on the proven BMW all-independent suspension and chassis, and is designed to evoke images of great past BMWs like the 507 roadster of the '50s. BMW wisely introduced the larger 189 hp 6-cylinder engine as an option earlier this year, satisfying complaints from those who felt the original 4-cylinder version was underpowered. Now the Z3 can run with the rest of the pack attaining 0 to 60 in the mid 6-second range. Along with this larger engine came some aggressive (and more attractive) body panels, including a larger grille and rear flanks. The Z3 flaunts muscularity, and with a base price of $35,900 it is aggressively competitive at the market as well.

To summarize, this roadster is a sports car for loyal BMW customers as well as for folks ready to step up into something more than mere mass transportation. It's also much like the Porsche. In typical BMW fashion this car delivers a tactile, satisfying drive that is sure to please.

Best New Porsche: The Boxster

$39,980 (list)

The all-new Porsche Boxster is perhaps the "purest" sports car of the four. It incorporates a mid-engine design along with one of the best-handling chassis and tire combinations in the world. This car, unlike the 911 series (which in earlier years was a difficult car to control when pushed), is most forgiving and will in most instances keep even a bad driver out of trouble.

Appearance-wise this is a gorgeous vehicle with a pure and simple form that still retains many of the best Porsche styling cues from the past. The Boxster's exterior and well-executed interior design have not disappointed the legions of Porsche loyalists. One look and you know it's a Porsche. In an important deviation from the past, its all-alloy 205 hp, 2.5-liter flat-6 engine is water-cooled. The engine proves itself a more than adequate performer, with 0-to-60 acceleration in the high 6-second range and a top speed of 149 MPH.

To summarize, the Porsche Boxster is a classic sports car in the truest sense that is the most forgiving, easy-to-drive Porsche ever and perhaps, with the top down, the most handsome of the four.

Best New American Car: Corvette C-5

$39,995

The first time I drove this car my impression was *Wow!* Now that I've had it for a while, all I can still say is *Wow!*

Until this year, Corvettes have been recognized as powerful sports cars for people willing to make some sacrifices in the ride department and the "fit and finish" area. This has all changed. The new Corvette C-5 inherited almost no components from its predecessors, while at the same time bearing a very strong family resemblance (stylewise) to its Corvette ancestry.

The C-5 has already earned a reputation for great value and it is well built, extremely fast, and devoid of the many rattles and squeaks that plagued earlier Corvettes. Huge tires and great brakes coupled with a taut suspension allow this 3,230-pound machine to handle like a race car. The big aluminum 346-cubic-inch engine generates 345 hp; this, along with the smooth aerodynamic design of the body, allows for an ungoverned top speed of 172 MPH and an acceleration rate of 0 to 60 in under 5 seconds. The gobs of torque produced by the big V8 engine deliver a seamless rush of power at almost any speed.

Those annoying swirls of colored lights that were intended to be futuristic-looking speedometers and tachometers have been, thankfully, banished. In place of this gaudy display, the new dash is almost all analog with large, easy-to-read gauges and a handsome classic interior design. The deep step-in has also been greatly reduced, making the sometimes-difficult maneuver of entering and exiting Corvettes a thing of the past. The car reminds me of a "take no prisoners" American muscle car. However, it is also blessed with enough refinement to appeal to those folks who, until now, have only been satisfied with European or Japanese quality.

The Corvette C-5 is by far the fastest of the four best picks, possessing more brute power and subtle refinement than ever before. The C-5 marks the beginning of a renaissance for Corvette and is a true American sports car that can compete on virtually every level with almost any vehicle produced anywhere today. Yes, that even includes Ferraris! Chevrolet should be proud.

Best New Mercedes: SLK

$39,700 (list)

It may be the smallest Mercedes, but the new SLK is literally guaranteed to turn heads, especially when its hard top is in the process of going up or down. This car was designed from the very start to be a hard-top convertible. This is not a "chop top" like so many nonfactory custom convertibles. It utilizes factory-engineering techniques that produce a convertible without the usual compromises in body rigidity. The car is absolutely squeak- and rattle-free and feels as though it was crafted from a solid billet of steel. The one-touch button makes the all-metal top disappear into the trunk in less than half a minute!

In true Mercedes tradition, the SLK is brimming with just about every safety feature known to man. The surprise is the price: just $39,700. The limited supply (7,000 for the U.S.) sold out ten months before the car was even formally introduced, and people are buying "delivery position" from other customers in order to get SLKs as soon as possible.

Both the interior and exterior are styled with elegant simplicity, for a look much like the SLK's more expensive siblings. It is more of a "sporty" car than a "sports" car. On the sporty side, it does come equipped with a supercharger that provides anything but docile performance. The engine produces 185 hp and propels the vehicle from 0 to 60 in 6.7 seconds. This car provides the luxury for which Mercedes Benz is noted, along with the security of a real hard top.

The Mercedes Benz SLK combines the best of all worlds: sports and luxury, hard top and convertible, all in one vehicle. The SLK is at home at the club or twisting around a fast country road. This is the most youthful and fun car Mercedes has ever built and is the making of yet another legend in the Mercedes tradition.

Best Car Security Device: Mobile Security Communications CarCop

$800

If you buy one of the afore-mentioned cars, you'd better get a security device too. Although most cars these days include some type of security device, there is one after-market kit that promises to deliver the highest level of protection ever.

Called the CarCop, this system is an all-encom-passing car security, personal navigation, and electronic key-finder all in one package. Using a cellular phone, GPS satellites, and around-the-clock monitoring provided by the world's largest home security company, ADT, this is the most versatile system I've ever seen.

For $800, CarCop installs a cellular phone and GSP satellite tracking box in your car. You are assigned a code number that you press when you enter the car. If someone tries to steal the car, CarCop automatically alerts ADT operators that the vehicle has been taken without authorization from the driver. ADT tracks the vehicle via satellite, contacts the owner, and dispatches the authorities.

CarCop also features a valet-service mode that when activated, automatically disables the cellular phone and notifies ADT if the vehicle is driven more than two miles. Its service mode has a ten-mile automatic call when you place your car in a service station. So if you've ever wondered if your car is being joy-ridden while you are dining at a fine restaurant or while it's in the shop for service, this system will put an end to the mystery.

Options include a remote locksmith service which, by calling an 800 number, can automatically unlock the car's doors 24 hours a day 7 days a week. There's even a friendly vehicle locator option that allows you to locate a family member simply by placing one call to ADT.

BOATS

Did I mention that I have the greatest job in the world? I get to not only test out the latest in computers, audio/video systems, and kitchen products, I also have the pleasure (and yes, it is a pleasure) of reviewing things that float—boats, personal watercraft, and luxury yachts. Although this requires traveling to cities like Miami every February for the Miami International Boat Show and the Brokerage Yacht Show, I seldom complain. After all, would you rather travel to a snowy New York City to work in the *Today* show studio, or go to south Florida and bask in the sunshine in midst of winter?

This section features the best of the best in numerous boating categories. So, if you have a little cabin fever, and are looking for a cure, just grab that Hawaiian shirt and a pair of sunglasses and read on.

Best Boat Motor Trailer: Bayliner Capri 1850 SS

Under $15,000

The first boat you buy will be the most important. That's because if the experience is good, you'll be hooked for life. If not, you will live up to the old proverb "The happiest days of a boatowner's life are the day he buys it and the day he sells it."

In order to avoid falling into this category, you must first determine what will you be using the boat for. If you like to fish, and buy a ski boat, you will not be happy. If you like to ski, and buy a cabin cruiser, the same could be true.

To keep my advice consistent, I have to say that it is wise to start small and work your way up or, because boats usually depreciate quickly, save some money and start with a used model. You can also start with a new all-in-one BMT (boat, motor, trailer) value package and get a lot of bang-for-the-buck.

This year's hot BMT package is Bayliner's Capri 1850 SS. This is an 18-foot-long model that features comfortable seating for five with enough room left over for storage of coolers, life vests, and water skis. It includes a 3.0 MerCrusier, 4-cylinder low-maintenance inboard-outboard engine that is powerful enough to pull a skier even when it is loaded with gear and passengers. It weighs in at just 2,300 pounds and can be towed by just about anything short of a Hyundai. But the main attraction to the Capri 1850 SS is its price. At under $15,000 for everything, it can be just the ticket to taking a lake vacation every weekend of the summer.

Best Personal Jet Boat (Tie): Yamaha Exciter TwinJet 220 and Sea Doo Challenger 1800

Each $17,000+

The first time I drove a personal jet boat, I couldn't believe it. Spawned from the personal watercraft industry, these fiber-glass-hulled wave skim-mers deliver more fun for the dollar than anything I have ever driven.

Based on a personal watercraft's impeller-type engine, these models bypass the propeller and gain their power by blasting high-pressure water from the stern of the boat.

Generally speaking, personal jet boats are shorter than most boats and feature rounded hulls and comfortable cushioned seats, but best of all they deliver the same ease of use and turn-on-a-dime maneuverability and per-formance of its personal watercraft cousin. Because of new hull designs, personal jet boats are able to jump over waves and can accomplish an exhil-arating 360-degree sliding turn with the flip of the wheel and an adjustment of the throttle—definitely not for the faint of heart!

This new category of boating is so exciting and both Yamaha and Sea Doo have introduced state-of-the-art designs, both will share the award for this category.

The Exciter and Challenger both feature 220 hp inboard engines. Sea Doo's model is bigger, 18 feet long, and holds up to seven passengers while Yamaha's is 16.7 feet long and holds up to five passengers. Both are also ideal for pulling skiers.

Both jet boats feature ski storage, built-in coolers, and because of their lightweight watercraft engines and hulls, they can go places no other boat can even attempt to go—you can even pull them up on the beach. The bottom line is if you're in the market for a family recreational boat, check out these jet boats before you buy.

Best Day/Overnighter Boat: Wellcraft Eclipse 2400SC

$35,230

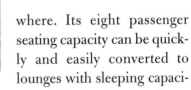

With top speeds up to 52 MPH and a cruising range of about 173 miles, this 24.4-foot boat is great for day trips to a secluded island or for an overnighter just about any-where. Its eight passenger seating capacity can be quickly and easily converted to lounges with sleeping capacity for up to three adults. With an 8.6 beam (width), there is virtually no feeling of claustrophobia, and the boat includes an entertainment and refreshment center with built-in cooler storage.

Other features include a full-featured control panel and a head—which means a bathroom for you landlubbers. It is powered by a MerCrusier 5.7 LX I/O engine and is trailerable. Because of Wellcraft's reputation for quality, this is an excellent buy for the mid-level market.

Best Way to Get Audited Boat: Palmer-Johnson Marine

$12 million+

If money were no object, and you could buy anything in the world, this would definitely be on your wish list. Sized a mere 150 feet long, 27 feet wide, and with more than 10,000 square feet of living space, this luxury yacht is one of the finest in the world.

In February 1997 I had the pleasure of hosting a live *Today* show segment from this beauty and the only difficult part was leaving. Once I was onboard, I quickly learned the definition of luxury—and this is it. Although the model I was on was outfitted with four master suites, a huge living room, a dance floor, and a dining room table that seated 12, a purchaser of this caliber could have the yacht custom designed to his or her needs. This one was equipped with a huge galley (kitchen) that is larger than most homes, crew quarters for 12 mates—yes, it takes almost that many to keep this baby afloat—and two 2,000 hp engines that can take this beauty from sea to shining sea at a swift 20 knots.

Although it starts in price at $12,000,000, you could easily add a few more millions to its price tag with custom features. But if the price tag scares you, just think about the sales tax. Or, if any of your friends offer to pay for gas—let them—as it holds a whopping 16,750 gallons of fuel.

PERSONAL WATERCRAFT

Although the name "Jet Ski" belongs to Kawasaki, the world associates it with those fast, fun water-motorcycle-type devices that skip across the water at super speeds. To make sure we are all singing off the same sheet, let me fill you with the proper names for these items.

A Jet Ski refers to the models that instead of allowing you to sit, like a motorcycle, allow you to stand. Of all the models on the market today, these units require more strength and stamina to control. That's why they are so popular on the water racing circuit.

The sit-down models are referred to as personal watercraft, and they are exactly what its name implies—a personal watercraft vehicle.

Allow me to add that I think that riding these things without a life-jacket is not only dangerous, but also illegal in most parts of the country. Although a high-speed fall will most likely not leave permanent damage to your body, it could leave you wishing you had a lifejacket. Not wearing a lifejacket can be equated to not wearing a helmet while riding a motorcycle. *It's just plain stupid!*

When shopping for a personal watercraft, first-time buyers should be cautioned not to go out and buy the fastest, most expensive model on the market. Like a motorcycle, these higher-end models can be more difficult to learn to ride and equally hard to master. The entry-level models, on the other hand, are easy to mount from the water and can provide countless hours of fun. When it comes to children riding these units, be sure to check local laws for minimum age requirements and make sure that youngsters do not ride without parental supervision. Also, not all lakes allow for the use of personal watercraft. Your boat dealer should be able to provide a list of where personal watercraft can be ridden safely and legally. Since many of the models include a safety video, take the time to watch it—it will teach you things about your specific model that could keep you from being stranded in the middle of the lake.

Best Family Watercraft: Kawasaki 1100STX

$7,500

On the entry-level side of the fence is this model from Kawasaki. What makes this Jet Ski from Kawasaki the best on the market is its ability to carry three passengers comfortably without sacrificing power.

Now the whole family can ride instead of standing on the shore waiting for a turn. Even better is its 120 hp engine that allows you to tow water-skiers and tubers.

Other features include a rear open deck for storing ski gear and ropes, a retractable rear boarding step that makes getting on a Jet Ski easier than ever, and a large 14½-gallon fuel tank for longer trips.

Best Muscle Watercraft: Sea Doo XP

$7,500

With a unique hour-glass-shaped hull design and two passenger capability, this 110 hp easy-to-operate "muscle" machine from Sea Doo delivers racing performance.

What's better is that Sea Doo has refined its suspension to give you the smoothest ride available in personal watercraft. And if speed is what you need, even though the manufacturers won't tell you (lawsuits, you know), this puppy has been clocked at speeds over 60 MPH. Aesthetically, this machine shines as well, with an all yellow detailing that will definitely turn heads.

Best Speed Personal Watercraft: Yamaha WaveRunner GP 1200

$8,000

Each year the competing personal watercraft companies up the ante by adding more and more power and speed to their watercraft. Unfortunately, I believe this one-upmanship will eventually hurt the industry as more and more lakes and resort areas are banning personal watercraft from its shores due to injuries.

However, for many customers, speed, not brand names, is what counts, and this year's speed demon is Yamaha's WaveRunner GP1200.

Featuring a 135 hp engine, this machine will not only flat-out move but at speeds over 70 MPH it may peel your eyebrows off too!

Other features include 11.4 gallons (more than any other two-seater) of multistorage space, room for two riders, a five-position quick-shift trim system for more precise handling and control, plus a space-age instrument panel with the industry's only digitally programmable locking ignition for security. It also includes a speedometer, a clock, side-mounted adjustable mirrors, and an extra-large 13.2-gallon fuel tank.

SNOWMOBILES

While John and I agree on most things, when it comes to snowmobiles we are snowdrifts apart. I prefer the luxurious comfort of larger machines, while Kelley prefers muscle machines with speeds of more than 100 miles an hour.

During our last snowmobile *Today* piece in Maine, our differences came to a head with Kelley zooming at Mach 1—refusing to share his Yamaha VMAX 700SX with the rest of the crew, while I basked in the comfort of my Ski Doo refusing to give mine up as well.

However, a compromise has been reached as two snowmobiles have been chosen as best of the year.

Best Comfort Family Snowmobile: Ski Doo Grand Touring SE $8,900

This is the Gurumobile loaded with all the bells and whistles.

What makes this the ultimate luxury snowmobile? First off, heat. This two-person machine not only heats the driver with thumb warmers and a leg heat vent but has passenger heat vents as well. Second, it has the best suspension in its class with a 10-inch-long travel rear suspension guaranteeing comfortable rides over even the most difficult terrain.

Performance-wise, it packs a powerful 699cc liquid-cooled engine, has an easy electronic start, hydraulic disk brake, and a reverse gear. Other features include a windshield design that keeps the wind off both you and the passenger, built-in saddlebags, and storage space for all your gear including a luggage rack. It even has an electronic antitheft system.

Best Speed Demon Snowmobile: Yamaha VMAX 700SX

$7,100

This snowmobile is for aggressive riders only, as it delivers the highest speeds and best suspension on the market.

During testing, Kelley consistently clocked speeds of more than 100 MPH. It literally flew across the snow. It features a 3-cylinder 698cc liquid-cooled engine, a lightweight chassis, and excellent suspension provided by long tapered trailing arms for superior strength and handling.

The only thing faster than this snowmobile is the drop in your bank account when you buy it at $7,100.

CHAPTER 7

Timepieces and Potpourri; or, Stuff that Didn't Fit in Other Chapters

As you can tell by the contents of this book, the Gadget Guru staff works overtime covering the world of new products. From consumer electronics, computers, and software to motorcycles, hardware, and cars, we cover just about everything on a category-to-category basis. But sometimes, we find products that don't fit into a specific category—they stand out on their own. Some may call them misfits, others conversation pieces. Interested? Read on.

WATCHES

Best Conversation Timepiece: Seiko Kinetic

$285

When I worked as a sales manager for Texas Instruments more than twenty years ago, I got to see the watch industry convert from an analog to digital industry almost overnight. Today, there is hardly anything a watch can't do—including delivering the time of day. But one of the most unusual, if not technologically advanced models on the market, is Seiko's Kinetic watch. This model, instead of using a mainspring or battery as a power source, generates its own power.

Like the self-winding models of yesteryear, all the Kinetic needs to keep going is movement. The simple motion of brushing your teeth or washing your hands generates enough energy to power the watch for 5 hours. Just wearing the watch for 10 hours of normal movement provides enough energy for 3 to 7 days of use. Each Kinetic model features an on-the-dial indicator that displays exactly how much energy is stored, and when the power is running low it will signal the user by causing the second hand to move in two-second increments. Seiko's Kinetic series of battery-free watches is available in both men's and women's styles.

Best Alternative Energy Watch: Pulsar Solar
$165

It seems like just about every major manufacturer, at one time or another, has attempted to take on a "green" image by delivering products that are either comprised of recycled materials or ones that bypass batteries and electricity and gain power from the sun. The problem is, very few of them succeed. Pulsar's new solar-powered watch is an exception to the rule.

Located on the dial of this sleek timepiece is a tiny solar panel that converts light into power. A mere nine minutes of bright sunlight delivers enough power for a full day. Three hours of sunlight will fully charge the watch's internal battery and power it for six months. So at least you can accomplish something other than a tan during a day at the beach. Even better, the Pulsar Solar can also be powered by artificial light. This is definitely one to watch (pun intended)! It is available in men's and women's styles.

Best Sports Watch: Timex Ironman Triathlon with Data Link System

$70 (includes software)

This watch not only keeps time but keeps appointments, phone numbers, and training data as well.

Designed to work with Windows 3.1 or 95–based computers, Timex's Data Link System is a companion software package that comes with the watch and allows you to transmit information wirelessly from your PC. It's really cool.

To use just enter phone numbers (up to 38) and personal information including daily, monthly, and yearly appointments, anniversaries, and reminder alarms into the computer program, put the watch in communications mode, and hold it in front of the computer. A series of flashes transmits the data from the computer to the watch in about five seconds. A button on the watch and digital display allows you to scroll through the information on your watch.

What's best about the Ironman with Data Link is that the software is customized to include targeted sports applications such as times for soccer, basketball, football, or other more personalized modes like countdown timers for workouts.

Of course the Iron Man is great for workouts, as it has a 100-hour chronograph with lap and split timers, a 50-lap memory recall for best lap calculations, an Indiglo night-light (the brightest in the business), and is water-resistant to 328 feet.

Best Watch for the Next Two Years: Branco CountDown Watch

$80

Did you know there are less than 1,000 days until the year 2000? The countdown watch does. That's because this analog watch not only tells you the time, it comes preprogrammed to count down the seconds digitally until the year 2000. On its watchface are three brightly colored globes including the sun, moon, and earth and a small rectangular indentation that displays how many hours, minutes, and seconds left until the biggest New Year's Eve party of a lifetime.

A great gift for the anal-retentive, the watch is waterproof to depths of 90 feet and comes with a leather band. And when your two years are up you really don't have to throw it away. The watch can be programmed to count down anything (e.g., pregnancies, anniversaries, etc.)

Best Money-Eating Watch: Ulysse Nardin Astrolabium Galileo Galilei

$76,000

From the sublime to the ridiculous comes a watch that not only displays the time of day, but places a complete guide to the solar system on your wrist as well. It features built-in electronics and a five-handed watch face complete with astrological mapping that measures and displays the altitude of the sun over the horizon, calculates the seasons, the movements of the zodiacs, foretells eclipses, and tells time and day too. Hey, for this kind of money, they should throw in a telescope.

ALARM CLOCKS

Best Alarm Clock for Kids: RCA AM/FM Stereo Clock Radio Model No. RP-3601K9

$35

Yes, you can buy your child a standard clock radio—but what fun would that be? That's probably what went through the minds of those wacky folks at RCA when they introduced this model. Colored bright red, yellow, and blue, this is the perfect accessory for any youngster's nightstand. It features

a large, easy-to-read bright-red LED digital display and an AM/FM radio. Also, for those early schooldays it has an oversized, hard-to-miss snooze button right on its top. And so they can't use it as an excuse to be late, it has a battery-backup feature that triggers whenever the power is disconnected.

But best of all, it includes a miniature plush version of RCA's mascot's offspring, Chipper.

Best Alarm Clock: Oregon Scientific Time Machine

$100

If you are sick and tired of having to reset your clock every time daylight saving time comes in or out of play, then this is the clock for you.

That's because Oregon Scientific's Time Machine automatically sets and resets itself when needed. Concealed behind its exterior is a tiny radio receiver that is tuned to the U.S. Department of Commerce's National Institute of Standards and Technologies' Atomic Clock. The Atomic Clock sends out signals six times each day that are picked up by the Time Machine's antenna that not only synchronize the time to the exact second, but the date as well. Even better, it automatically adjusts for daylight saving time and for leap year—meaning that you'll always know what time it is. Its LCD display is a pleasant blue for easy nighttime reading.

POTPOURRI

Best Gift for the Cigar Aficionado: Tombow Havana Pen

$50

Cigars are trendy. From generation X-ers to senior citizens to men and women, it is now a fashion statement to stop off at the cigar bar for a smoke with your pals. But what if you don't smoke and want to make a fashion statement? Then this novel, but functional, product is for you.

Sized and shaped like a fancy cigar on the outside, inside is a roller-ball cartridge that delivers a smooth smoke—make that *stroke*. This pen features a wide, well-balanced barrel and comes packaged in its own metal case complete with a realistic-looking cigar band. So if you are looking for a gift for the smoker or the nonsmoker on your gift list, this could be just the ticket.

Best of all, you'll never be told to sit in the No writing section.

Best James Bond Pen: Machina Pencorder Soma

$80

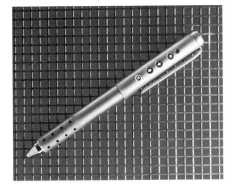

This sleek ballpoint pen can not only help you write down your thoughts, it can record them too.

Built into the pen is a tiny computer chip that can record up to 75 seconds of messages. Although admittedly, you may look strange, or be mistaken for Maxwell Smart talking to your ballpoint pen in the office corridor, you'll certainly never lose that moment of inspiration that always seems to come at the most inappropriate times.

Located on the pen's side are forward, reverse, record, erase, and playback buttons. You can play one memo at a time or skip forward, back, and repeat memos as well. You can even recover erased information. The Pencorder is available in a sleek black metallic or stainless steel design.

Best Voice Organizer: The Voice It Manager Model No. VM-30

$165

The problem with most digital (tapeless) voice recorders is twofold: They are only able to record a few minutes of dictation, and the voice quality makes it sound like you are talking underwater.

Voice It's dictation-length voice recorder not only combats those ills, but is now packed with new features that make digital voice recorders worth a second look.

For those not familiar with digital technology, a digital recorder is in many ways similar to a pocket tape recorder. However, instead of recording the messages on tape, it records onto an electronic chip. And unlike a tape recorder, these devices allow you to instantly access or erase messages without the bother of having to search with fast-forward or rewind.

What separates the Voice It Manager from the pack is that instead of just a few phrases, it allows for up to 30 minutes of high-quality monaural recording on its 8 MB memory. But allow me to note that although I consider the voice quality on this machine higher than other electronic recorders, it is not up to par with even the most basic tape-based recorder.

But the Manager has many other features that a tape recorder does not, including a file management system, a telephone directory, and an alarm.

The Voice It Manager is compact and easy to operate. It is about the size of a pocket calculator and weighs just 4 ounces. An LCD screen at the top (2x¾ in.) displays all the functions on the unit plus the day, date, and time.

One of the most practical features is the categorizing system, which allows each message to be placed into your choice of five different files. This facilitates the often frustrating chore of finding a specific message. The categories can be labeled from its library of 16 icons. It has such headers as things to do, meetings, and expenses, or you can create your own file name just by pressing record.

Messages are stored in memory until you purposely erase them, so there is no danger of inadvertently recording over important notes. The flash memory chip is designed to retain all information even when battery power is lost.

Also included is its personal telephone directory. It enables you to enter and retrieve a phone number and automatically dial it just by pressing play. By holding the Manager up to the telephone mouthpiece, the tones are generated, thus eliminating the need to manually dial the phone number. It can hold approximately 100 names with three phone/fax numbers for each.

You can also attach voice messages to the telephone directory entries. This can be used for remembering titles, addresses, and notes about the person that you're calling.

It also includes a calendar/scheduling option that features an alarm. It enables you to prerecord and set an alarm or message to play automatically at a specified time. So if you have a doctor's appointment, you can program the alarm to go off when you are supposed to leave. You can even attach a memo reminding yourself not to forget the insurance papers. Recurrent reminders can be recorded just once and scheduled to play back regularly by day, week, month, or year.

One feature I found to be especially important is the confidential file, which requires an access code for entry. This is practical for users who store personal information and would also come in handy if the unit were ever lost or stolen.

For those who carry the Voice It Manager in a pocket or purse, there is a function that prevents the unit from operating unintentionally. The lock option will freeze all the functions until it is unlocked for further use. The unit is sized $4\frac{1}{8}$x$2\frac{1}{2}$x$\frac{1}{2}$ in. It comes with 3 AAA batteries, which will last four to six months, depending on usage. The microphone and volume control are located on its front while the speaker is on the back.

VIDEO GAMES

Best Video Game System: Nintendo64

$199

If you love video games, run, don't walk, to the store and purchase the Nintendo64. This is the best video game system on the planet.

Way back in 1994 we previewed this system in Chicago and were excited about it then. But it took nearly two years of delays before Nintendo finally delivered this 64-bit cartridge-based game system. In the meantime, both Sony and Sega introduced CD-based game systems, and quite frankly, we wondered if Nintendo was going to be too little too late. Boy, were we wrong. Nintendo flat-out smoked the competition, selling out way before last year's holiday buying season.

Unlike its predecessors, Sony's PlayStation and Sega's Saturn, which store and play games from a CD, the N64 bucked the trend and stayed with the more tried-and-tested solid-state cartridge format. (No, this unit is not compatible with the existing Nintendo cartridges.) Although cartridges do not have the storage capacity of CDs, they grant faster game play and speedier level-to-level movement that result in better game play.

The N64 also incorporates anti-aliasing technology (co-developed with Silicon Graphics) that enhances game play by preventing the jagged edges and flickering movements associated with CD-based games. This technology, combined with real-depth buffering, allows game developers to efficiently create 3-D environments with enhanced visuals that dwarf those of the other game systems.

The N64 system includes a three-grip controller that facilitates 360-degree precision movement. This allows the on-screen characters to perform previously unheard-of maneuvers such as running in circles. It also incorporates new buttons that change the player's perspective and grant new levels of game involvement.

Although the game console is the first to feature built-in connectors for up to four controllers, only one controller is included. Additional controllers sell for $30 each.

Best Video Game TV: Samsung GXTV

$350

If you are serious about video games, or know someone who is, then you'll surely want to take a look at Samsung's new GXTV.

Billed as the ultimate video game monitor, this 13-inch television features a pair of built-in 21-watt speakers, a 15-watt subwoofer, and preset game sound

settings that add a new dimension to game play. Even better, its oversized speakers fold inward to protect the screen when not in use.

For better viewing the monitor is mounted on a swivel base and includes on-screen displays as well as multiple video inputs for the connection for up to two different video game systems.

Allow me to note that this unit is also a 181-channel cable compatible television and includes a remote control.

CHAPTER 8

Travel Products

For some of us, traveling is a way of life. I, for one, spend as many days on the road (or in the air) as I do in my Nashville office. Therefore, I am constantly in search of new items that make travel less taxing.

LUGGAGE

Today's generation of luggage is lighter, more space-efficient, and better designed than ever. And just about every piece on the market includes what I feel is the greatest innovation to roll through the terminal: *wheels!* The inclusion of wheels on luggage makes any size bag easier to transport, all but eliminating the need to search for a Skycap in a busy airport.

Best New Concept "Collapsible" Luggage:
Travel Pro Snap Roll

$465

This entry from Travel Pro is a bit different from those of years past because it not only features wheels, a concept invented by Travel Pro, but it is collapsible too.

Called the Snap Roll, this model can be transformed from its standard 10-inch thickness to only 5 ½ inches in a matter of seconds. This allows the luggage to be stored under a bed or out of the way when not in use, and makes it ideal for those who want to bring an extra bag in which to stash purchases made while on a trip.

The Snap Roll comes in two sizes and includes a retractable handle.

Best Wheeled Luggage: Tumi Wheel-A-Way

$475

Tumi is also entering the expandable arena with its new soft, expandable carry-on bag, the Wheel-A-Way. The 22x14x10 in. piece features a front panel pocket that expands up to 3 inches to accommodate additional clothing or last-minute items.

In my testing I've found Tumi to be the easiest carry-on bag to pull through airports. Instead of using standard plastic wheels, Tumi bags use the same type of wheels found on better-quality in-line skates. This allows you to maneuver over a variety of surfaces with a minimum of effort, even when your bag is loaded to capacity.

Best Idea Luggage: Eagle Creek Cargo Switchback

$290

One of the most unusual if not unique new luggage designs is Eagle Creek's Cargo Switchback. What separates this model from the pack is that not only can you roll it from place to place, you can also wear it.

Concealed behind a foldaway panel are backpack-style shoulder straps that allow you to carry the bag in places where standard wheeled luggage doesn't like to roll, such as on stairs, gravel driveways, or the narrow aisles of an airplane.

The bag is 20x14x8 in. and weighs 6.1 pounds. It fits into an airplane's overhead bin.

Best Big Luggage: Samsonite E-Z Cart

$150

Samsonite's new rolling wonder is the E-Z Cart. Designed to be checked as baggage, this upright bag features an innovative, four-wheel design that allows it to rest at an angle and be pushed, pulled, or pivoted almost effortlessly.

Because the bag rests on four wheels as opposed to two, the weight is borne by the suitcase, not by the person pulling it. Inside, it boasts special shelves that enable you to stack and pack items in an orderly, wrinkle-free fashion. A strap allows other bags to be fastened to the piece, and either left- or right-handed pullers can use the unit's handle.

Best Garment Bag: Athalon Sky Valet

$300

Those seeking an easy-to-maneuver hanging garment bag will surely want to check out this bag, which has to be the most versatile on the market today, as it stands, folds, wheels, and hangs.

Unlike garment bags that need to hang in a closet to be packed and unpacked, this one has a built-in spine and extensible legs that allow it to stand freely anywhere. Clothes can be packed on hangers and you don't have to fold the bag to carry it. Wheels and a handle allow it to be rolled in its upright position through the airport and hung in a standard airplane closet.

Not only do its platform legs allow it to stand in place, they also let you piggyback another carry-on bag. But like other garment bags, the Sky Valet can be folded and placed in a car trunk, checked as baggage, or pulled on its wheels.

TRAVEL ACCESSORIES AND DOODADS

Best Travel Curling Iron: Braun's Style Shaper Cordless Curling Iron

$30

This unit is ideal for travelers because instead of a big bulky cord, disposable butane cartridges power it.

Great for the morning commute or cab ride to a meeting, each cartridge fully heats in about 90 seconds and provides about a month's usage. You can only bring three of these cartridges on an overseas flight.

It comes with a special cover that enables you to slide it in a bag immediately after use. Cartridges sell for $7 for a double pack.

Best Travel Blow Dryer: Travel Smart Mini Cyclone 2000

$25

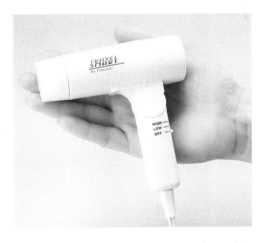

Look at the front cover of this book and you will easily see that I have no use for a blow dryer. That is until Travel Smart developed this unit.

Called the Travel Smart Mini Cyclone 2000, this tiny blow dryer fits in the palm of your hand. But don't let its small size fool you, because it delivers a powerful 1,200-watt blast of hot air. More than enough for people with lots of hair or just a few hairs like me. Best of all, when folded it can fit in a shirt pocket or purse.

Best Overnighter Product: Stuffed Shirt Case

$110

If you've got a quick day trip or overnighter, instead of packing a big bag with nothing in it, check out the Stuffed Shirt Case.

This 11x9x2 in. handheld case is designed to hold a folded dress shirt, underwear, cuff links, jewelry, and a tie. Its outer zip pouch is ideal for toiletries and a razor as well.

Best Travel Alarm Clock: Braun's Voice Control Travel Alarm Clock

$40

With many hotels slacking in the wake-up call department and providing antiquated alarm clocks, the best way to ensure you do not miss that morning meeting is by carrying your own travel alarm clock.

Braun's voice-control unit is simply

the best. It features a unique voice-activated snooze function; to silence this alarm, all you have to do is just *yell* at it. This triggers the voice-control mechanism, which silences the alarm for eight-minute intervals. This snooze cycle will continue until you reach over and turn the alarm off. Other features include an illuminated dial, analog clock face, and a handy built-in penlight.

It runs on 1 AA battery and sells for $40.

Best Traveler's Watch: Jeager-LeCoultres Reverso Duo

$6,250+

This is the ultimate travel watch, as it features the world's only back-to-back dials.

On one side you can have New York time and the other London. When you get to your destination just flip the watch face over and you have the local time. Flip it back, and the other side maintains perfect "home" time. The analog watch has a classic design and separate second hand dials. It operates off a single mechanical movement and is dressed to kill with a sleek black watch face on one side and a white on the other. It comes with a leather band and costs roughly as much as two round-trip Concorde tickets: $6,250.

CHAPTER 9

Coming Attractions: Best New Technologies of the Year

Flat televisions and hi-fi speakers that hang on your wall, VCRs that rent movies for us, tapeless camcorders, and organizers with built-in cellular phones and digital cameras: These are just a few of the new technologies that will be clamoring for your attention over the coming year.

Of course, many new technologies are what the industry calls "vapor ware"—meaning now you see it now you don't. So in an effort to distinguish fact from fiction, we've assembled what we consider to be the best and most likely to succeed technologies of the year.

Best New Television Technology: Plasma

$ a lot

A number of manufacturers including Mitsubishi, Sony, Panasonic, and NEC have been previewing plasma, or flat-panel televisions for the past couple of years.

Although plasma TV sounds more like something on *ER* than something you watch *ER* on, these revolutionary new sets operate on a combination of gases, which are heated to produce color pictures. This eliminates the big bulky cathode-ray tubes, or CRTs, found in traditional

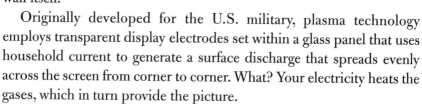

monitors, allowing plasma TV sets to be less than 4 inches thick—so you can literally hang these units on your wall or, in some cases, have them built into the wall itself.

Originally developed for the U.S. military, plasma technology employs transparent display electrodes set within a glass panel that uses household current to generate a surface discharge that spreads evenly across the screen from corner to corner. What? Your electricity heats the gases, which in turn provide the picture.

Thousands of phosphor dots within the screen's surface, each representing a primary color, become active with the charge and produce a true-to-life full-color image that contains 64 levels of gray and reproduces up to 167 million individual colors.

Because the dots are fixed and spread evenly across the screen, the image doesn't have the corner distortion that occurs with standard picture tube and projection sets. It also allows for a 160-degree angle of view. Unlike televisions with tubes, plasma screens emit no radiation so they can be safely viewed from any distance.

Cost? Well plasma TVs are not for the faint-of-wallet as a 21- to 42-inch model will sell for anything from $10,000 to $25,000. Like any new technology, look for prices to come down as the manufacturing costs become lower as demand increases.

Best New VCR Technology Announcement: edd (Electronic Digital Delivery)

Move over Blockbuster, competition is just around the corner. It's called edd (electronic digital delivery), and it will most likely change the way we rent or purchase movies, music, and even video and computer games in the near future.

Developed by a company called Emc-3, edd is a feature that will be incorporated into future VCRs. In fact, as of press time more than 15 VCR manufacturers have already announced their commitment to this technology.

Here's how it works:

To find a movie, you will just press a button on your remote control and select a category from the on-screen menu. Depending on your setup, you could place your order by clicking on the menu, by accessing Emc-3's Internet site, or by contacting them via telephone. Then, just place a blank videotape in your VCR and kick back and wait while the movie you selected is electronically delivered to your VCR. Depending on the length of the movie, the download process will take about five or ten minutes. The rental price, which is promised to be about the same as that of a standard video store fee, allows you to view the movie twice, then, like they say in *Mission Impossible*, it will automatically self-destruct. This means that no return trip to the video store is necessary, and there will never be another late fee.

The reason it will take only a few minutes to copy is that edd is a digital system and will be using a compression technique that copies the movie at high speed. But since the tape in the VCR is traveling at the standard speed, it will only occupy a small space on the tape itself. This brings up a small hitch.

The edd system will not work with today's analog VCRs—but it will with the next generation of digital VHS models. Or, if those units are delayed, it can be made to work with other digital storage mediums such as a computer hard drive, the mini-disk, or the future recordable DVDs.

Before you start bypassing the video store though, let me say that the edd feature is not yet available on any VCR. Although it is promised to start showing up sometime in 1998, allow me to be skeptical and say that I will be thrilled if it shows up by then.

Regardless of the timetable, this could be the best new technology to hit the VCR since the auto clock set feature eliminated the flashing 12:00 syndrome. Edd is expected to add about $100 to the price of a VCR.

Best New Speaker Technology: NXT Flat Panel Speakers

Proving that when it comes to audio the world may soon be flat, NXT technology's new wafer-thin, less than 1-inch-thick flat-panel speakers are prepared to shake up the audio world.

The first products on the market should come from UK speaker giant Mission, whose prototype flat speaker home-theater setup, which even had a flat center channel speaker built right into the projection screen, wowed a private audience in Las Vegas earlier this year.

Aside from the obvious benefits of wall-hanging speakers, NXT has also managed to maintain the ever-important audio "sweet spot" in its products that true audiophiles demand. This allows flat panel speakers to sound as good or better than the high-quality existing speakers.

Best of all, the manufacturing process is said to be less expensive than building big bulky speakers, so one can only assume that this technology will, after its initial roll out this year, become an affordable and efficient way for consumers of the future to enjoy audio.

Best New Technology Camcorder: Hitachi MPEG-1A

$2,600

If you are looking for proof that technology gets better each year, then look no further than the world's first tapeless camcorder from Hitachi.

Dubbed the MPEG-1A, this tiny marvel records its images on a miniature hard disk drive much like the one in your computer. Other than recording up to 20 minutes of movies, this model also has the capability of taking and storing up to 3,000 digital still images at a resolution of 704x480 pixels. It can also record up to 4 hours of digital audio recording—or a combination of all three formats.

This technological marvel allows for playback and editing on either a television or a computer—and since the images and sound clips are digital, they can be electronically transmitted over phone lines.

The Hitachi is a mere 5⅜x3⅓x2⅙ in. and weighs 19 ounces—making it noticeably smaller than existing camcorders. It is equipped with a 6X zoom and a 1.8-inch color LCD monitor for framing and playback.

Best New Desktop Computer Monitor Technology:
NEC MultiSync 20.1-inch LCD Monitor

$8,000

LCDs, like the aforementioned plasma TV monitors, require very little desk space, as they do not need a bulky CRT to distribute images.

Although the LCD screen is standard on many high-end laptops and pocket organizers, this year marks the first time LCD technology is being offered for the home desktop computer.

In a nutshell, LCD technology incorporates a process whereby an electric charge stimulates tiny liquid crystals that are packed together between two glass panes, to produce color images on screen. Aside from saving desk space, these monitors consume up to 50 percent less power than conventional monitors do.

Until LCD manufacturing becomes less expensive, LCD monitors will continue to cost up to 50 percent more than comparable CRT monitors, so it's best to wait out this emerging technology.

But if you just can't wait, then feast your eyes on NEC's MultiSync 20.1-inch LCD monitor. With a new technology that allows for complete 160-degree viewing of the LCD screen (which many LCD designs don't have) this ultra-thin, 4-inch-thick monitor delivers up to 1,280x1,024 resolution and the brightest pictures you've ever seen on a computer monitor. Oh, but did I mention it sells for $8,000?

Best New Modem Technology: Cable Modems

No matter where you turn, somebody's talking about the Internet. But once you've gotten past all the hype and the deals of the week, the one thing all Internet users can agree upon is that it is S-L-O-W.

I, for one, do not know how the term "surfing" came to be connected with the Internet. After all, when you surf television channels, a click of a remote control instantly takes you from one station to another. On the Internet, however, once you have entered a specific site's address, you have to wait and wait and wait—in some cases more than a minute—until the desired image comes fully into view.

This is not surfing—it's more like dog-paddling through rough seas. The Internet is so slow because it is delivered to your computer over standard telephone lines.

Although today's state-of-the-art modems travel at speeds of up to 56 kbps and are lightning fast compared to those models of yesteryear, they're still not fast enough to bring high-quality graphics onto your computer screen in a timely manner.

You would think that faster modems would be on the way to cure this ill. Well, they aren't—or, at least, no one is talking about them. That's because today's phone lines aren't capable of transmitting data much faster than 56 kbps. And until fiber optics are in place, which probably won't happen until well into the next century, that's as fast as it gets.

One way to speed up the process is by installing an ISDN line, which allows for transmission speeds up to five times faster than conventional phone lines and is provided by the phone company. The problem with ISDN lines is that they are expensive (about $200) to install. They cost about $30 per month to maintain, and they require a dedicated modem that costs another $500.

A noticeably faster method is to use a satellite to deliver the Internet to your home. But although satellites operate about 50 times faster than today's modems, they can only receive data, they cannot transmit it. You will still need to connect your computer to a phone line in order to send commands to the Internet and jump seamlessly from page to page. Satellites are also very expensive, with prices starting at around $800, not to mention installation and monthly service fees. Companies such as Hughes have new products that combine a satellite modem with a DSS receiver, enabling users to connect one system to both a television and computer.

But don't worry, a definitive answer appears to be just around the corner, and it's called a cable modem. Believe it or not, the cable that is already wired into 70 percent of today's homes is capable of transmitting and receiving data and graphics at a rate of more than 1,000 times the speed of a 33.6-baud modem. That's fast enough to allow us to truly surf the Net, going from page to page in seconds—about as long as it takes to change channels on a television.

There are two types of cable modems: two way and one way. A two-way cable modem will be usable in areas that have been "rebuilt"—equipped with fiber-optic cables that lead from the cable company to "nodes," or junction boxes, that are strategically placed throughout the coverage area. This will allow users to connect a cable modem to a computer, send and receive commands, and view Web pages as well as full-motion video at lightning speed.

For those who don't live in a rebuilt area, there is another solution—a one-way cable modem that, like the aforementioned satellite system, will send the signal to the Internet via a phone line and download it via the cable. Although this system is not as fast as a two-way cable modem, it will still deliver the information hundreds of times faster than today's technology.

The good news is that all this speed is not as expensive as you might think. The cable modem itself will sell for about $500 upon introduction, and will most likely come down quickly in price. The service is expected to cost around $20 to $30 per month—about the same price currently charged for the slower telephone-line services.

Best New Concept Organizer: Nokia 9000 Communicator

$1,000

As the commercial says, "Someday, you'll be faxing from the beach." Well, that someday is here now, if you have the right equipment. But how about a product that allows you to send and receive faxes, make phone calls, retrieve e-mail, surf the Net, and do just about everything except wash the dishes from anywhere?

Nokia's new 9000 Communicator can do all that—and more. But, not in the USA—at least not yet. At first glance, the Communicator looks like a standard cellular phone, only a bit larger. It is hinged and opens up to reveal a small but very functional keyboard and screen, like a pocket organizer.

The Communicator enables the user to perform a wide variety of tasks without wires or cables. You can type in a letter and fax it to any destination with just the press of a button. You can also use the

Communicator to transmit and receive e-mail, access the Internet, and (similar to some pocket pagers) send and receive short messages.

Additionally, the Communicator serves as a personal organizer. It has separate buttons for contacts, notes, and calendar functions. And it also provides a built-in speakerphone.

But what separates the Communicator from the pack is that all the applications work together. It enables you to receive a note silently during a business meeting, copy it to a word processor, send it to a fax machine, and call to discuss it while reading it on the display.

The Communicator features a 4¾x1½ in. grayscale LCD screen on the organizer and a smaller 1½x1¼₀ in. illuminated LCD screen on the phone. Incoming messages appear on the screen you are working on. It is powered by a 24 MHz Intel 386 processor and includes 8 MB of memory—6 MB allocated to flash and 2 MB for user data storage.

It is also IRDA-compatible—meaning that data can be exchanged wirelessly between other similarly equipped units. The Communicator provides up to 120 minutes of talk/fax/data time or 30 hours of standby time per charge. But although one battery powers both the phone and computer, the data is kept in a nonvolatile memory and will be maintained even when the battery is completely drained.

But here's the bad news: Because the Nokia 9000 Communicator is designed to work with a digital mobile-phone network called PCS (personal communications service) it will not operate on existing cellular phone systems. PCS is just starting to be developed in the U.S. and due to competition and the technology, it will be years before PCS is universal. Also, there are a number of PCS derivative services competing to be the standard of this industry. PCS may be the phone service of the near future, however, as its advantages over cellular are numerous: handsets will be lighter, batteries will last longer, it will grant Internet access as well as simultaneous voice and data transmissions. Unlike cellular towers, PCS antennas are smaller and less intrusive. They can be blended with the landscape and even disguised as trees. Also of note is that PCS phones use smart cards containing microchips, allowing encrypted subscriber information that promises to reduce fraud and theft.

The bottom line is the Nokia 9000 Communicator is the first of many products to come that will blend a number of useful functions in one easy-to-use unit. It is definitely a technology to keep your eye on.

Best Organizer for James Bond: Sharp Model No. MI-10DC
$1,200 to $1,300

Straight out of the pages of a 007 script, Sharp is taking its popular Zaurus pocket organizer/computer to a new level with the addition of a slide-in digital camera as well as Internet browsing capabilities. This combination of features allows users to compose and send a fax, store all your names, addresses, and phone numbers, take pictures, transmit them to others, and surf the Net all on one device. Whew! All of these images can be viewed on its 5-inch color backlit screen.

The camera, which slides into the side, will enable you to capture up to 90 still images in its 2 MB memory—granted, if you store that many photos, you won't have room for anything else.

When the unit is in camera mode, the other functions temporarily disappear and allow the images to be composed and viewed on its color screen. The images can be transferred to a computer via a cable or infrared wireless transmission or e-mailed via the Internet.

This same screen also allows for full-color viewing and surfing of Internet Web pages. Although the unit has a built-in albeit super-slow 2,400-baud data modem (9,600-baud fax transmission speed), it can accommodate a faster 33.6 PCMCIA modem ($200). If you can afford the unit, you can buy the faster modem.

It is 4 $\frac{1}{10}$ x6 $\frac{4}{5}$ x1 $\frac{1}{5}$ in. and weighs 17.3 ounces and will sell for $1,200 to $1,300.

Best New Appliance Technology: Horizontal Axis Washing Machines

If you took a normal washing machine and turned it on its side and removed the agitator, then you would have this revolutionary new concept in cleaning called Horizontal Axis.

Destined to be the hottest news in appliances since the Brady Bunch got one of those refrigerators with a built-in water dispenser, horizontal axis washers use 40 percent less water than traditional machines, a feat made possible by the absence of a beater bar: Instead of turning your clothes, the machine gently rolls them in less water in a preferred horizontal motion that produces cleaner clothes.

Expect to see units from every major manufacturer including Frigidaire and Maytag costing only $200 more than traditional units.

CHAPTER 10

Postcards from the Road

$\mathbf{B}$ringing the world of new products to you on a regular basis means logging hundreds of thousands of miles on airplanes each and every year. It seems that we are always traveling to some trade show, industry announcement, or attending a factory line showing.

This also translates into thousands of rubber chicken dinners, schmooze and booze cocktail events, and the obligatory press conference featuring a less-than-exciting engineer/product manager or hotshot MBA marketing exec exclaiming why his or her product is the greatest thing since sliced bread. Unfortunately many of these line showings include more baloney than meat and are nothing more than a way for manufacturers to keep their names in front of the working press. But such showings are necessary evils, as you'll never know when they just might introduce something that could truly change our lives.

To survive the trade show circuit, and maintain a little sanity, we've developed an eclectic taste for some of the best attractions on the road. While we're no travel guide, we do have enough frequent flyer miles to be dangerous.

ROLLER COASTERS

For the past seven years, I have been the designated roller coaster expert on NBC's *Today* show. While I'm not entirely sure if the NBC execs periodically send me to cover new roller coasters out of respect for my crack (if not unorthodox) reporting skills, or if they have some sadistic plot in mind, but I can tell you that I have become something of an authority on thrill rides. The best part of reporting on the latest, greatest, and fastest coasters on the planet is that I never have to stand in line—park management always sneaks me in the back door. One day, however, when the Batman ride was opening at Six Flags in New Jersey, the crowd started to become a bit angry at me and my crew for cutting in line. I guess that was because the only thing bigger than the ride itself was its long line. So, when the folks in line started with their comments, I just introduced myself as a safety inspector and told them I was investigating a suspicious sound. You would not believe how quickly the mob's raspberries turned to thanks. Maybe I have a little Jon Lovitz in my character—yea, that's the ticket, just making sure all the bolts are tight!

My most hair-raising moment on a coaster was in 1996 as NBC *Today* had the exclusive morning show coverage of the opening of the Stratosphere in Las Vegas. This is the roller coaster that was built around the top of Vegas's newest skyscraper, the Stratosphere Hotel and Casino. To tell the truth, this coaster was a wimp. It was slow, no great g-forces, and featured no amazing dips or dives. But, what made it interesting, if not dangerous, was that it was not completely finished at the time I was doing my report. In fact, it took two trips and three delays just to board it. Needless to say, the PR folks were embarrassed.

This coaster, the High Roller, circles the outside top perimeter of the building three times. My crew had wired a tiny camera and video recorder to the seat in front of me. My job was to ad-lib a commentary that could be used in the taped portion of the segment. Well, on the first lap around the building I felt a big "clunk" and the car felt like it was about to fall off its tracks. Something was not right. The goods news for me was that my car did not start careening forty-some-odd floors toward the desert, but continued to go around in circles. But boy, when something like this happens, you won't believe what goes through your mind. I immediately changed my commentary to a video recording of my will. Willis, the audio engineer, was monitoring the audio through a wireless device and when I arrived at the stopping point, he was laughing so hard I thought he was having a heart attack. I still think he has a copy of my forced last will and testament and probably will use it against me at a future date. That's why it's always important to be real nice to the crew, buy them dinner, make sure they get the good hotel rooms and all the right perks. After all, you never know when they are recording what you are saying. Nonetheless, this was my best hair-raising coaster experience, although this coaster was a real dog. For real thrills here are the best coasters in America:

Best Amusement Park to Satisfy Your Coaster Craving: Cedar Point

When I was contacted by *Today* show producer Roland Woerner and told that we were going to make television history and put together the world's first live network broadcast of a moving roller coaster, I was thrilled. What an opportunity! Until this point, any coverage of roller coasters seen on television was taped—not live. At that time Cedar Point had the world's largest wooden roller coaster in the country (maybe the world, but my memory is not that good). Why did we need a wooden coaster? Because we knew it would be next to impossible to get a microwave signal out of a metal coaster as it would bounce just about everywhere—except toward the receiver. A wooden coaster, on the other hand, gave us half a chance of success. To make a long story short, it worked. Even with the clunking and tossing around, we gave the world the first look at an unedited coaster adventure. Katie and Bryant and even Al Roker thought I was nuts. Hey, I was just having fun.

Cedar Point is located on the Lake Erie peninsula midway between Cleveland and Toledo in Sandusky, Ohio. If you are a coaster junkie, this is the best theme park to visit. This thrill ride park features 12—count 'em 12—roller coasters including the Mantis, a killer scream machine that features 6 different elements.

What's unique about the Mantis is that you ride it while standing as it takes you on four upside-down inversions and a spooky 60 MPH 137-foot drop at a 52-degree angle that will literally convert you into a praying mantis.

Best New Roller Coaster: Superman the Escape

Located at Six Flags Magic Mountain Resort in Valencia, California, Superman the Escape is the best new coaster ride of the year.

This ride is not only the first ever to reach 100 MPH, it does so in less than seven seconds—that's almost two seconds faster than a Porsche Turbo Carerra. Unlike most roller coasters that twist and turn, the Superman ride consists only of an L-shaped, 1,315-foot track. To ride, you board a 15-man car and hold on to your eyebrows as the initial 100 MPH accelerates you straight ahead on a 600-foot track and than angles straight up 415 feet in the air. When you reach the top of the tower you experience an unprecedented 6.5 seconds of weightlessness before slowly beginning a 92 MPH free-falling descent. After riding this coaster 30 times all I can tell you is that although the total ride experience is only one minute long, it is outrageous.

Best New Concept Ride: SkyCoaster

The SkyCoaster is a combination bungee jump, skydive, and free-fall. When I opened the new SkyCoaster at Nashville's Opryland theme park, I rehearsed my segment at least 15 times—all before 6 A.M. Okay, for obvious reasons, I skipped breakfast that morning.

Truly an engineering marvel, the SkyCoaster consists of a 173-foot steel arch (sizes vary according to location) with an aircraft cable tethered to the apex of the arch. Between one and three riders are loaded into an aircraftlike suit and are hoisted up 15 stories (150 feet) where they remain perched until they are instructed to pull a rip cord. Once the rip cord is engaged, riders experience a bungeelike free-fall for about 50 feet, then the tethered cable lifts up and by some law of physics you suddenly level out and zoom upwards, floating like a pendulum, before returning to the launchpad. It's truly an exhilarating and comfortable ride.

SkyCoasters are located in more than 30 cities in the U.S., including the aforementioned Cedar Point and Nashville's Opryland and, of course, Las Vegas.

Best Burger: In N Out

Los Angeles may be best known for its trendy restaurants with tiny dressed-up portions and California cuisine, but the one restaurant that John and I stop by every time we get to the City of Angels is In N Out Burger. This is a regional fast-food chain with the best burgers in the country.

Silently mocking the McDonald's and Wendy's of the world with its limited menu, In N Out only offers two choices: a hamburger or a cheeseburger or double-double versions of both. All burgers are made fresh to order and served in diner-style wax paper by employees who really seem to like their job. Here is a tip known only by In N Out insiders. When you order a double-double cheeseburger tell them to "make it an animal." You'll get treated like royalty and it's the best burger you'll ever eat. Don't forget to wash it down with a vanilla milkshake!

Best Las Vegas Hotel: Caesars Palace

In a town that reinvents itself every six months, Caesars Palace remains the ultimate hotel in town. That's because instead of the bigger is better mentality, Caesars puts as much into its guest services as it does its casino. This translates into a quality stay with room service that arrives on time, five newly designed luxurious swimming pools, and the Forum Shops—an attached mall that not only features the best mix of stores anywhere, but restaurants such as Spago, Bertolini, and The Palm. After more than twenty years of attending trade shows in Las Vegas, I can tell you from good authority that when it comes to hotels in Vegas, Caesars is the best. Even better, it is one of the few hotels with a fast-moving cab line.

During your stay at Caesars make sure you say hello to Nick Mazola, the most famous card dealer in the world. This is the guy who had cards thrown at him by Joe Pesci in the movie *Casino*, and dealt to Dustin Hoffman and Tom Cruise in *Rainman*. He even has a part in *National Lampoon's Vegas Vacation* and has dealt me a few blows as well.

Best Products for the Recycle Bin

As you can imagine we see some pretty silly products here at the Gadget Guru. Here are our top five worst products of all time:

- **doggy water:** flavored bottled waters (fish, meat) for your pet. Really!
- the **Candom:** a condomlike rubber device that fits over your 12-ounce cold drink.
- **3DO:** a video game system with more than 300 titles, but not one winner.
- the **telephone blender:** yes, a blender with a phone attached.
- a **car alarm** that doesn't ring or make noise; no, this system, when activated, fills the car with smoke—lots of smoke. In fact, enough smoke to make Cheech and Chong proud. Are you wondering what happens if it is accidentally triggered while you're driving? So were we, and that's why you're reading about it here.

Phone Contacts

For questions, Web links, and updated information on the entire product listing in the book, go to:

http://www.gadgetguru.com

CHAPTER 1.
CONSUMER ELECTRONICS

8X8: (888) VIEW8X8
Aiwa: (800) 289–2492
Bose: (908) 233–8800
Cambridge Soundworks: (800) FOR–HIFI
Canon: (800) OK CANON
Casio: (310) 618–9910
Cidco: (408) 779–1162
Contax: (908) 560–0266
Denon: (201) 575–7810
Echostar: (303) 799–8222
Epson: (310) 782–4113
Ericsson: (919) 472–7000
Faroudja: (408) 735–1492
Fisher: (818) 998–7322
Fuji: (914) 789–8100

GE: (800) 211–3089
Go-Video: (602) 998–3400
Infinity: (818) 407–0228
JBL: (800) 645–7484
JVC: (800) 252–5722
Magnavox: (770) 821–2400
Marantz: (630) 307–3100
Minolta: (201) 825–4000
Mitsubishi: (800) 828–6372
Motorola: (847) 576–5000
NHT: (800) NHT–9993
Nokia: (818) 288–3800
Nortel: (800) 4NORTEL
Panasonic: (201) 392–6415
Philips: (770) 821–2400
Pioneer: (800) PIONEER
ProScan: (800) 336–1900
RCA: (800) 336–1900
RCA: (800) 211–3089 (Home Director)
Remote Blocker: (800) 866–6753
Rockustics: (800) 875–1765
Samsung: (201) 229–4000
Sanyo: (818) 998–7322
Sharp: (800) BE SHARP
Sherwood/Newcastle: (714) 521–6100
Sony: (800) 222–SONY
StarSight: (800) 643–STAR
Sybil: (603) 926–7688
Telalert: (317) 575–0700
Telectra: (317) 575–0700
Telemania: (800) 354–8785
Terk TV: (516) 543–1900
Toshiba: (800) 631–3811
TYCO: (800) FOR TYCO
Universal Director 8: (216) 487–1110
WaveCom RF-Link: (888) 273–5465
Yamaha: (800) YAMAHA
Yashica: (908) 560–0266

CHAPTER 2:
HOUSEWARES

Auto Chef: (800) 217–1958
Bissell: (416) 453–4451
Black and Decker: (203) 926–3000
Braun: (617) 596–7300
Brother: (800) 276–7746
BumpaBed: (800) 241–1848
Capresso: (800) 767–3554
CharBroil: (800) 352–4111
Conair: (201) 575–1060
Cosco: (812) 372–0141
Cuisinart: (800) 726–6247
Drinkwell: (800) 805–7532
Equator: (800) 935–1955
First Alert: (708) 851–7330 (bath seat)
First Alert: (800) 392–1395 (nursery monitor)
Franklin Wrapper: (800) 480–2610
Frigidaire: (800) 374–4432
Gino's: (800) 272–5629
Hansgrohe: (800) 719–1000
Keg A Cue: (800) 232–5347
Kirby: (800) 437–7170
KitchenAid: (800) 422–1230
Larosta: (212) 989–5219
Litter Maid: (800) 344–4444
Max Burton: (800) 272–8603
Maytag: (800) 688–9900
Metrokane: (800) 724–4321
Mr. Coffee: (216) 464–4000
Norelco: (800) 243–7884
Peek's: (415) 986–8895
Proctor Silex: (800) 851–8900
Rowenta: (617) 396–0600
Royal Dirt Devil: (800) 321–1134
Rubbermaid: (216) 264–6464

Safety Can: (800) 995–9511
Salton: (800) 272–5629
Sanyo: (818) 998–7322
Saving Pet Light: (800) 835–9899
Sharp: (800) BE SHARP
Sunbeam: (800) 621–8854
T-Fal: (201) 575–1060
Toastmaster: (800) 947–3744
Umix: (888) 864–8649
Vintage Enhancer: (800) 217–1958
Virtu Flex: (800) 656–2695
Wahl: (815) 625–6525
Waring: (203) 379–0731
West Bend: (414) 334–2311

CHAPTER 3.
HARDWARE

Bemis: (800) 558–7651
Black and Decker: (203) 526–3000
Contech: (800) 767–8658
Craftsman: (800) 377–7414
Deluxe Lite-Driver: (800) 769–1396
Dremel: (414) 554–1390
Echo: (800) 432–3246
Lasko: (800) 394–3267
Murray: (800) 224–8940
Poulan: (800) 554–6723
Roto Zip: (800) 521–1817
Rubbermaid: (216) 264–6464
Ryobi: (800) 525–2579
Telesteps: (800) 821–8388
Zircon: (408) 866–8600

CHAPTER 4.
COMPUTERS

Adobe: (800) 833–6687
Advent: (847) 317–3700
APC: (401) 289–APCC
Apple: (800) 776–2333
AST: (714) 727–4141
Audio Highway: (408) 255–5301
Berkeley Systems: (510) 540–5535 (You Don't Know Jack)
Brother: (800) 284–HELP
Canon: (800) OK CANON
Casio: (800) YO CASIO
Citizen: (800) 477–4683
Compaq: (800) 345–1518
Day-Timer: (800) 235–7355
Epson: (800) 463–7766
E-Z Legal: (305) 758–2476
Fieldworks: (612) 947–0856
Gateway: (800) 846–2000
Hewlett-Packard: (800) 322–4772
HotOffice: (888) 4HOT–OFF
Hughes: (301) 428–5500
IBM: (800) 426–7235
Iomega: (800) MY STUFF
Jump Piano Discovery: (415) 917–7460
Lexmark: (800) 358–5835
Living Books: (800) 521–6263
Mangia: (704) 357–1080
Microsoft: (800) 613–6103
Minolta: (201) 825–4000
Monorail: (888) 494–9501
NEC: (800) NEC INFO
Nokia: (818) 288–3800
Okidata: (800) 654–3282
Panasonic: (201) 392–6415

Princeton: (800) 747–6249
Psion: (508) 371-0310
Quicken: (800) 624–8742
Sharp: (800) BE SHARP
TravRoute: (800) 297–TRAV
U.S. Robotics: (415) 237-6000

CHAPTER 5.
SPORTING GOODS

AD One: (415) 401–7463
Coleman: (316) 832–2653
CSA: (800) CSA–0136
Dolomite: (800) 257–2001
Elan: (802) 863–5593
K-2: (206) 463–3631
Magellan: (909) 394–5000
Minolta: (201) 825–4000
Panasonic: (201) 348–7799
Rollerblade: (612) 930–7000
Salomon: (800) 225–6850
Schwinn: (800) 843–2453
Tough Traveler: (800) GO TOUGH
Zap: (707) 824–4150

CHAPTER 6.
BIG TOYS FOR AGING BOOMERS

Bayliner: (800) 233–3327
BMW: (800) 831-1117
CarCop: (770) 582–6710
Corvette: (800) CHEVY-MI
Harley-Davidson: (800) 443–2153

Honda: (800) 847–HRCA
Mercedes-Benz: (800) FOR MERCEDES
Palmer-Johnson: (800) 940-7642
Porsche: (800) 822-2476
Sea Doo: (514) 532–2211
Suzuki: (714) 996–7040
Wellcraft: (941) 753–7811
Yamaha: (714) 761–7800 (motorcycle)
Yamaha: (800) 442–2282 (boats)
Yamaha: (800) 4–YAMAHA (personal watercraft and snowmobiles)

CHAPTER 7.
TIMEPIECES AND POTPOURRI

Branco: (800) 528–7445
Machina: (800) 223–4340
Nintendo: (206) 882–2240
Oregon Scientific: (503) 639–8883
Pulsar: (800) 848–3545
RCA: (800) 336–1900
Samsung: (201) 229–4000
Seiko: (800) 848–3545
Timex: (800) FOR TIMEX
Tombow: (800) 835–3232
Ulysse Nardin: (212) 757–7030
Voice It: (800) 478–6423

CHAPTER 8.
TRAVEL PRODUCTS

Athalon: (888) SKY VALET
Braun: (617) 596–7300
Eagle Creek: (800) 874–1048

Jeager-LeCoultres: (212) 840–0888
Samsonite: (800) 262–8282
Stuffed Shirt: (800) 788–3333
Travel Pro: (888) 741–7471
Travel Smart: (203) 723–6664
Tumi: (800) 322–8864

CHAPTER 9.
COMING ATTRACTIONS

EDD: n/a (Europe only)
Hitachi: (800) HITACHI
NEC: (800) NEC INFO
Nokia: (800) 666–5553
NXT: n/a (Europe only)
Plasma: (800) 332–2119
Sharp: (800) BE SHARP